How To Grow Weird And Wonderful Plants

Paul Temple

Illustrations by David Mostyn

D1586034

Beaver Books

A Beaver Original
Published by Arrow Books Limited
17–21 Conway Street, London W1P 6JD

An imprint of the Hutchinson Publishing Group

London Melbourne Sydney Auckland Johannesburg
and agencies throughout the world

First published 1985

Set in Linoterm Bembo by
JH Graphics Limited, Reading

Printed and bound in Great Britain by
Anchor Brendon Ltd, Tiptree, Essex

ISBN 0 09 940960 7

Contents

Acknowledgements

I wish to thank the following people who helped me during the writing of this book: Mum, for checking the proofs; Dad, for teaching me the basics about plants; my brother, for helping find some of the suppliers; Sandra Banfield for doing the typing (and almost having patience); and finally, John Sirkett and all of the above for giving me suggestions for unusual plants. Thanks are also due to S.F. for listening to the idea in the early stages.

Introduction

If you would like to grow a strange plant this book will let you know the names of some of the most interesting and also how best to grow them. Of course, growing a plant can take a very long time, so you can also find out where you can get most of the plants described already fully grown. This is the best way to start until you have learned how to grow them yourself. In the meantime you can amaze your friends; even your parents will be interested in your collection. If you do not particularly want to grow the plants, do not worry. You can still read about all the amazing things that plants can do.

All plants have Latin names but sometimes they are difficult to pronounce. The trouble is that each country often has its own (common) name for a plant so one plant may have more than 100 names. Where it is helpful the best-known common name is given but it is always best to use a Latin name. Do not worry if you cannot speak Latin, but always try to use the Latin if you write to someone about the plant. For instance, do not write to a shop for a Dracula Plant, ask them for Sarracenia flava. As long as you can spell it you can be sure you are getting the right plant.

All the plants are easy to grow and should not die if you give them just a little care and affection. Plant societies will always give you advice if you have a problem and are well worth joining if you are really interested. If you are at all worried about your plant do not be afraid to ask for help from any gardener, especially the person who gave or sold you the plant.

7

Unfortunately, not all of the plants in this book can be found in nurseries or garden centres. Therefore, some plants are included which are probably only available as seeds but you may still wish to grow them. If you are interested in seeds you will need a lot more patience. They can take anything from a few weeks to several years before they even begin to grow. In some cases it may be several years before you have a large plant. The advantage of growing from seed is that it is cheap. You can get a large number of plants for just a few pence and if you have friends who grow plants this allows you to exchange some of yours for theirs.

Seeds are exciting. Even experienced gardeners continue to be amazed at how such small objects turn into large plants. When you plant seeds you never know exactly what you will end up with. They will probably all be the right plant but each one will be a little bit different. As a result, by pure good luck, you may produce a flower with a new colour, perhaps the first red snowdrop or a yellow-flowered Venus Fly Trap. So when you are ready, when you have the time, space and patience, buy a packet of seeds and watch as they turn into plants before your very eyes.

1 Smelly and scented flowers

For any of you who know how to cook, it will not be a surprise that some plants have a strong smell. Herbs and spices are all smelly plants but there are other even more interesting examples. Although we have learnt to use these to our advantage, the very strong smells are really to prevent animals from eating the plants. Think what it's like to eat raw onion!

Many plants, especially the ones we grow for pleasure, have flowers which are attractive. The flowers are often coloured but this is not so that we like them but so that insects or other animals will be attracted to them. Such a plant uses insects to pollinate the flowers so that seeds will be produced and a new generation of plants created.

Luckily for us, the flowers that attract insects are usually prettily coloured and have a pleasant perfume. However, some plants have taken advantage of the fact that insects also like the smell of rotting flesh! The flowers that produce this disgusting smell are usually very dramatic and always attract admiring comments from observers. Better still, these plants can be used to attract food for carnivorous (meat-eating) plants to catch.

The most incredible smelly plant also happens to be the plant with the largest flower in the world. Its name is Rafflesia and it is found in Malaysia where it is a parasite of vines. The flower can be as big as ½ m in diameter!

The Carrion Flower – Orbea or Stapelia

Stapeliads are a group of succulents. They are indoor plants, usually brownish-green and pleasant to look at. The flowers are often very strong smelling and with the Giant Carrion Flower, Stapelia gigantea (stap-eel-ee-ah jie-gant-ee-ah), it may be a test of courage to stay in the same room as the flowers can be up to 46 cm across and produce an enormous amount of 'rotten' odour. The Starfish Flower, S. asterias, and Variegated Carrion Flower, S. variagata, are both very popular and easy to obtain. In very modern books you will find that the name of these plants has been changed from Stapelia to Orbea. For example S. asterias would now be called O. asterias.

How to grow
It is best to grow stapeliads in a greenhouse although by a window will do. Keep your plant in a small plastic pot. Do not repot until the pot is full of

Carrion flower – Stapelia

roots, possibly once a year but probably once every
two years. When you think you need to repot, first
of all put on some gloves to protect your hands.
Carefully turn the pot upside down with your
fingers holding the soil around the plant. Tap the
bottom of the pot and when the plant falls out look
at the soil. If you can see lots of roots, repot into a
pot that is one size bigger than the old one.
Repotting is best done in March. (Gloves are really
only necessary for cacti but as many cacti look like
stapeliads, it is best to get into the habit of wearing
gloves.)

Water should always be warm rainwater and
must be given very carefully at the start of the
growing year. Just use enough to make the soil
damp and do this once towards mid-February (or
later if it is still really cold). Water, using just a little,

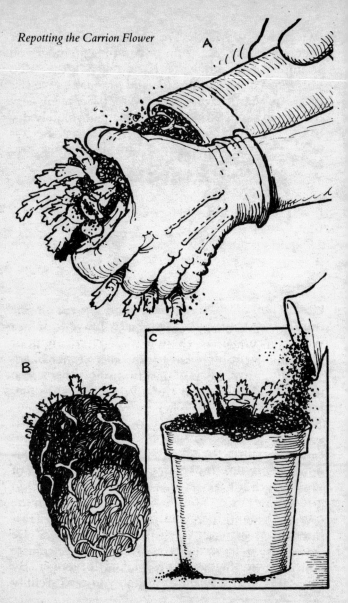

twice more in March. From April onwards, water every morning, but from July until September you should also add some cactus food. In September do not water unless it is sunny and gradually give less water until, in October, only water twice using very little each time. Now keep the plant absolutely dry until February. Remember that with succulents it is always better to water too little rather than too much.

Allow stapeliads as much light as possible all year. Keep them at 10°C (50°F) or more, but if they are hot in summer and cold (no less than 10°C) in winter they will flower regularly. From May to September, keep the windows open but prevent draughts as October approaches.

How to get more
Gently pull off one or two off-shoots or cut off one or two branches with a sharp knife. Leave them in a warm place to dry for two days. Hold the shoot or branch and push the cut or broken end into Sharp sand and treat like the parent plant. Repot into ordinary cactus mixture when roots have grown. Only do this in June or July.

Seeds can be grown too. In April or May fill a seed tray to two-thirds of its depth with damp cactus mixture. Pat it down gently. Sprinkle seeds over the mixture and cover them with a thin layer of soil. Cover the tray with a sheet of glass. Place in good light but do not let strong light shine on the tray and keep at a temperature of 22–25°C (71–77°F). If the glass gets wet on the inside turn it over. *Do not water*. The seeds should begin to germinate after one week but some will take a lot longer. By the following February or March you can carefully use a pin or needle to dig out each plant. Repot it in the smallest pot possible; then treat it like an adult.

Suppliers: Abbeybrook, Barleyfield

Lords–and–Ladies – Arum

This includes Britain's best-known member of a group of plants known as Aroids. It has many popular names including Fly Catcher and Starchwort but Lords-and-Ladies is the usual name. As with the other Aroids, flies are trapped to help with pollination. A fly, attracted by the meaty smell, is lured to the base of the flower hood. On entering through a narrow neck it must force its way through hairs which bend a little to allow the fly to pass down. Now the fly is trapped in a small area in which it moves about frantically trying to escape. Inside the 'trap' the male flowers are open and as the fly hits a flower some pollen is released. This covers the fly and also any flies that happen to be underneath the flower. After a day or so the hairs begin to die. Only now does the fly manage to escape. As the male flowers die the female flowers open. Flies covered in pollen will eventually enter another flower hood where female flowers are ready to receive the pollen and be pollinated. Perhaps accidentally some flies die and remain in the 'trap' but this is useful because, when they rot, all their goodness helps the plant to grow.

How to grow

Place a healthy plant outside in a soil that has some loam and a little leaf mould. Arums like shade so either plant it under a taller bush or find a place beside a wall that never gets full sunlight. A temperate climate will do everything else, but if the soil gets too dry you can give it some water.

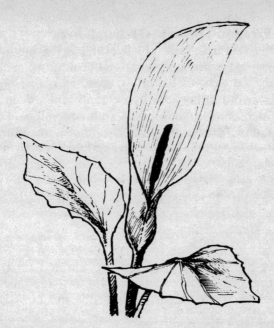

Lords-and-ladies – Arum

How to get more
If you leave your plant it will gradually form a clump by itself. Dig it up and pull apart the new shoots from the old plant. Either plant them separately or give some to a friend. The bright red berries can also be planted in the same soil, just below the surface, in early autumn. After spring, you should notice new plants beginning to pop up through the soil.

Suppliers: Avon Bulbs have several Arums but Garden Centres may be able to supply Arum maculatum, the British Lords-and-Ladies

The Dragon's Mouth – Helicodiceros

What a fantastic plant. Helicodiceros (he-lick-oh-diss-err-oss) probably got its common name because dragons, being strange and fearsome beasts, were thought to be evil and foul-smelling, especially their breath. Not only does the plant smell like rotting meat (and perhaps the putrid inside of a dragon's mouth), it also looks exactly like a large, rotten steak. An incredible choice for a flower, not particularly pretty, but it certainly is eye- (or should that be fly-) catching.

How to grow

This plant is very difficult to acquire, so as soon as you see it on sale, buy it. You will need a large flower-pot, probably about 30–33 cm in diameter. Fill the pot with ordinary soil, any reasonable garden or commercial soil will do, and bury the plant about one-third of the way down the pot. Planting should be done in spring or autumn. If you obtain a plant at any other time keep it in the dark, dry and not too cold (in a garden shed is perfect) until it is the correct time to plant it. In spring you can water it so that the soil is always moist. Keep doing this all through the growing season until the leaves begin to go yellow. Then gradually let the soil go dry and keep it dry until next spring. Most important of all, although this plant is meant to be hardy it can be damaged by frost. Keep it indoors until June and bring it back in after October.

How to get more

After a year or two you will see that your pot contains more than one plant. When it does, wait until October or November, dig it up and carefully break off any of the small plants which are known as 'offsets'. Treat the offsets in exactly the same way as the mature plants, but they will take several years to flower.

Suppliers: Avon Bulbs

Other Aroids
If you would like to try another aroid there are many to choose from. Most are even more dramatic and many are smellier than Lords-and-Ladies. Some smell quite nice. You can choose anything called Arisaema (a-riss-ee-ma), Arum or Dracunculus (drac-unc-you-luss). If you have a bit of garden near a warm wall or a place in a cold greenhouse, Dracunculus vulgaris is large, easy to grow and really evil-looking. Just use the same soil as above (nice and leafy) and keep the soil moist all year. Arum dioscorides is small but smellier and can be kept in the same way. Arisarum probiscidium (a-riss-are-um probe-iss-sid-ee-um) is positively ridiculous. Who would have thought that an aroid or any other plant could look like a mouse? It is a shame that many people do not know of it.

Suppliers: Avon Bulbs, P. J. Christian, Oak Gardens, P. Kohli, Valhalla

Thyme–Thymus
Lemon Thyme – Thymus citriodorus
This plant is not only unusual but you can eat it as well. Thyme is of course a very well-known herb used in kitchens all over the world. The usual type that you can buy, in bottles, in any food shop has an easily recognized taste that can add a bit of life to any meal. Lemon Thyme has a very different smell but still has the same taste so it adds a bit of extra interest

17

to the meal. To see how strong the smell is just take one or two of the tiny leaves in your hand and roll them about with a finger. Now smell your hand or finger. There are several different types of Lemon Thyme so the strength of the smell will depend on which one you have. Surprisingly, there are many plants that smell like lemons – you could even start a collection of them!

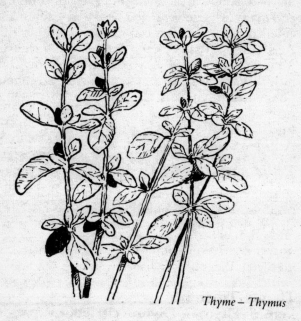

Thyme – Thymus

How to grow

Use any ordinary soil with added sand. Plant in full sun. Replant about every four years in small clumps, splitting up the large clumps by gently tearing them apart. Rockeries are excellent places to grow Thymus. Planting is best in late autumn or early spring.

How to get more

Divide large plants into small rooted clumps in spring. Alternatively sow seeds in ordinary soil, also in spring. Just cover them with a thin layer of sandy soil. You can take 6–7 cm cuttings, removing the bottom leaves and planting the bare stem in soil. Put in a greenhouse or plastic bag and keep moist. The cutting will root in a few weeks.

Suppliers: Sandwich Nurseries, Beth Chatto

Pelargoniums

Many gardeners find the Pelargoniums (pel-are-go-nee-ums) are really worth collecting. They are grown for their attractive flowers, interesting and unusual leaves or, of course, for their smell. Unfortunately, there are many people who like to call these plants Geraniums, so do make sure you use the correct name. There are so many scented Pelargoniums it would be silly to describe each one and how to grow it, so only some of them are listed below so that you will know which ones smell of what. The summary of how to grow them should prove suitable for most Pelargoniums. If you decide that these are the plants for you it might interest you to know that there is a society which can help you with advice, obtaining plants and anything else to do with them. The details are to be found in the section called 'Societies' on page 000.

Recommended plants are:

Pelargonium capitatum	rose-scented
P. citriodorum	lemon-scented
P. crispum	lemon-scented
P. fragrans	nutmeg-scented
P. radula	balsam-scented
P. tomentosum	peppermint-scented

How to grow

Pelargoniums are quite easy to grow successfully. Use a 12-cm pot filled with John Innis Potting Compost No. 1. Keep the soil damp all the time. When growth begins you can increase the watering if you like but the plant will still be happy if it is kept damp. If you do increase the water, start decreasing again when the leaves begin to turn yellow and die. You can grow these plants on a windowsill or in a greenhouse, but do not place them in strong, direct sunlight. Never let them be colder than 10°C (50°F), but if they are warmer than 15°C (60°F) keep a window or door (or both) open.

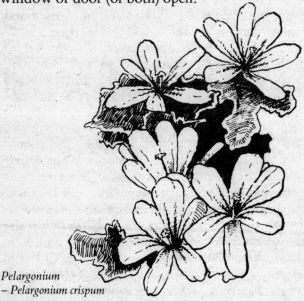

Pelargonium
– Pelargonium crispum

How to get more

Sow seeds in spring. They prefer a light, sandy soil at 12–18°C (55–65°F). Cuttings can be taken in autumn and should be placed singly in 5-cm pots. Keep them at 7°C (45°F) until spring and then move the cuttings to bigger pots as they grow. Use John Innis No. 1 for planting cuttings.

Suppliers: Beckwood Geraniums, Sandwich Nurseries

The Fish and Chips Plant – Monanthes

Of all the plants in the world, this is the one that is possibly the hardest to believe. It is an example of a group of plants that all store water in their leaves, stems or roots, all such plants being called succulents. A cactus is an example of a succulent because it stores water in a swollen stem and there are many interesting cacti that are worth growing. This plant is not a cactus and is fairly ordinary to look at; but it is not too hard to keep. It is greenish-brown in colour, including the flowers which look as if they are made of wax. But on a hot, sunny day, when the flowers are wide open, they smell of fish and chips! It is a very greasy smell that is hard to identify but when fish and chips are suggested most people immediately agree.

How to grow
Monanthes is best treated similarly to a cactus. Use any commercial cactus potting compost or any other potting compost with some sand added. In winter, keep the plant at about 4°C (40°F) but in summer it can be given as much heat and light as you like, and this will help stimulate the flowers to open and create the fish and chip smell. Water only occasionally in winter, perhaps as little as once or twice a month. In summer you can water generously each day.

21

How to get more

You can divide a large clump in half but it seems a shame to do so. A small cutting taken from a good plant can be painted with nail varnish (to cover the cut end) and put into a hole in the soil. Then treat it like the parent plant.

Suppliers: Barleyfield, Abbeybrook

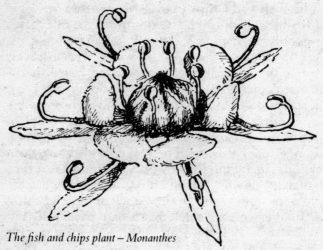

The fish and chips plant – Monanthes

The Hot Biscuit Plant – Peperomia graveolens

This is another really strange plant. Again it is a succulent, but this one is far more beautiful to look at and makes an excellent window plant. The fat leaves are green with a dark red underside, but the flowers are quite unusual being long thin spikes held high above the plant. Apart from its strange appearance, the flower also has an unusual smell. Once again it is strangely familiar but difficult to identify, until somebody tells you that it smells of hot biscuits.

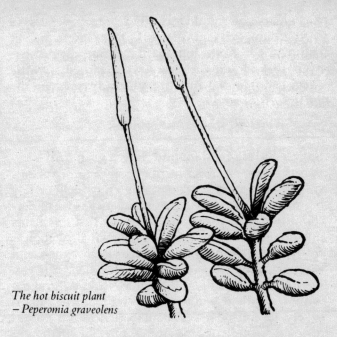

The hot biscuit plant
– Peperomia graveolens

How to grow

This is grown in the same way as Monanthes and
many other cacti or succulents. Use a commercial
potting compost (with added sand if it is not made
specially for cacti) and keep the plant at a minimum
of 4°C (40°F) in winter. In summer give plenty of
heat and light to help the flowers give off their
biscuity perfume. Water rarely in winter but often
in summer.

How to get more

A leaf cutting of Peperomia (pepper-oh-me-ah
grav-ee-oh-lens) should be the easiest way to reproduce this plant. Take a leaf and carefully break it off
the plant. If you have nail varnish paint the broken
end with it. If not, as with most other cacti and

succulents you should leave the leaf for several days so the damaged end dries off. Then insert the cut end of the leaf into some potting compost that has been soaked and then very well drained. A little extra sand in the mixture will help prevent the cutting from rotting.

Suppliers: Barleyfield, Abbeybrook

Sage – Salvia rutilans and Salvia grahamii

What is it that causes a plant to copy another plant's smell? Obviously it does not copy deliberately because plants do not have intelligence as we understand it. Equally obvious is the fact that the plants must gain an advantage from their smell. Well, it is really quite simple. Take a nice, fresh lemon and smell it. Now take a bite of the skin, just as if you were a hungry animal. Horrible, isn't it? So what would you do if you found a plant that smelt like a lovely lemon? After your experience you would probably think that anything smelling of lemon tastes horrible so you would leave it alone. Strong smells are a plant's way of warning animals not to eat them. Salvia rutilans (sal-vee-ah root-ee-lans) is a sage that grows 1 m high. Its leaves are scented and if you rub them between your fingers they smell of pineapple. S. grahamii (sal-vee-ah graham-eye) is a sage that grows to ½ m tall and smells of blackcurrant. Both smell really nice, especially if you put just one leaf in a nice cold drink.

How to grow

You can use most garden soils but an ordinary commercial potting compost will do. Both these Salvia species are tender which means you must keep them indoors or in a greenhouse in winter.

Water them whenever the soil feels dry. If a shoot seems to be too long use finger-nails to nip off the end. This will force the plant to be more bushy.

How to get more
Seed can be sown in spring. The soil should be kept moist either by careful watering or by covering the pot with a plastic bag. Cuttings can also be taken in spring or summer. Cut off a 6 cm length of shoot, dip the cut end in rooting powder and put it into a 3 cm deep hole in the soil. Now press the soil around it, and cover the cutting with a plastic bag for about three weeks. Finally, large plants can simply be cut into several smaller ones.

Suppliers: Sandwich Nurseries

2   Plants that eat insects

Surely of all the plants in the world these must be the
most famous. Surprisingly, only a few people grow
them, probably because very few of them know
how to. Now it can be seen how easy they are to
grow and everybody will be fascinated by them.
Plants that eat insects are called 'carnivorous' plants.
All of these plants tend to grow in places where the
soil is very poor. Because of this they do not get
much to eat, so the occasional fly or ant makes a
tasty meal which helps them to grow. The plants
can be beautiful or very bizarre to look at, and the
flowers are often very attractive and long-lasting.
There are plenty of different plants to choose from
and there are types for indoors, in the garden and
greenhouse.

The Venus Fly Trap – Dionaea muscipula

Not only is this plant carnivorous but it is also one of the fastest moving plants in the world. The leaves are specially designed to form a trap which snaps shut to imprison the prey and seal it in. Then the leaves press tighter and tighter while they empty a liquid into the trap which slowly digests the animal, letting all the goodness reach the plant through the leaves. Finally, the trap reopens to await the arrival of another unsuspecting dinner-guest.

Each leaf is specially modified by years of evolution. The leaf narrows at the end and then expands into two large pads. Along the edge of each pad are soft spines that act like prison bars when the trap is closed. Each pad is coloured red on its inner surface to help attract insects. Insects are colour-blind, but red appears darker to them than other colours. On the red side of the pad there are also three small hair-like structures. These are the triggers that cause the trap to shut, and mean almost certain death to whatever touches them. It is difficult to set off the trap. If you touch the tiny hair-like trigger just once the trap will stay open. Touch it or any two hairs twice, quickly, the trap will shut, but it will soon open again. Rain does not make the trap shut at all. Only food will shut it and keep it closed.

The Venus Fly Trap or Dionaea muscipula (die-oh-nee-ah muss-key-pew-la) is a native of Carolina in North America, but it is very rare in the wild and should not be collected. Many people sell plants but only good plants are easy to grow, so it is best to buy a plant from a recommended supplier. The traps should be at least 1 cm long, preferably bigger, if you are to be sure of a plant that will be easy to grow. This remarkable plant was so famous that it even made a guest appearance in the very first Dracula film, *Nosferatu*, made far back in 1922.

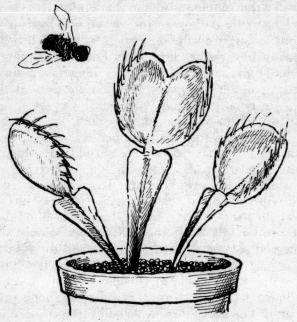

Venus fly trap – Dionaea muscipula

How to grow

Buy a mature plant. Take a 13 cm half-pot and fill it with a mixture of two parts peat moss and one part clean sand. Plant the Venus Fly Trap in this mixture. *Do not* use any sphagnum moss and do not cover the plant with anything. Always stand the pot in a plant saucer containing rainwater or distilled water. Do not use tap water; in an emergency you can use boiled tap water that has been allowed to cool, but do not continue to do this for very long. Keep the plant on a nice, bright, warm windowsill.

If any flowers begin to show, cut off the flower stalk as soon as possible. The flowers are not very pretty and if they start to produce seed they can weaken the plant too much. Do not worry if a leaf turns black and dies. All plant leaves die eventually on every plant. Only worry if all the leaves are beginning to turn black.

How to get more
If you treat the plant well it will produce new plants for itself. Every now and then dig up the plant and pull off the new ones, but they can look better left in a group. Seed takes a long time to grow into mature plants, so it is not a good idea to try growing from seed unless you have a few years to spare.

Suppliers: Sarracenia Nurseries, Marston Exotics, Peter Paul's, Plant Shops Botanical, Carnivorous Gardens, Hinode-Kadan, Millingimbi Nursery, New Dawn Nursery, Renate Parsley, Thysanotus-Seed-Mailorder, Harald Weiner

The Pretty Sundew – Drosera capensis, Drosera rotundifolia

This must be one of the prettiest sundews of all, and it is very easy to both obtain and grow. The plant is bright green with long flattened leaves. The leaves are covered in tiny red hairs and each hair ends in a tiny drop of a sticky substance that looks like dew. On a bright day, each leaf will appear to be covered by hundreds of tiny bright droplets each holding a rainbow. The bright purple flowers are pretty too.

All sundews are very good at catching flies or ants. The sticky drop on each hair acts like a bait because it is sugary. (Try some on your finger-tip if you dare!) When a fly tries to taste the liquid it finds that it is sticky. By that time, the fly is usually standing right in the middle of the glue. As it struggles to escape, its movements cause the whole leaf to bend over. The result is rather like a fly sandwich with the unlucky fly being slowly digested between two layers of sticky leaf.

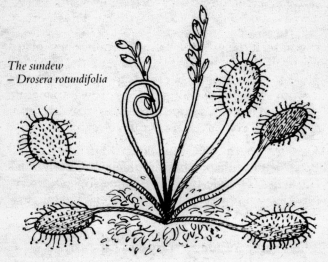

The sundew
– Drosera rotundifolia

How to grow
If you know someone who grows carnivorous plants, ask them for seeds as they are quick and easy to grow. Simply sprinkle them on the surface of the soil. Otherwise, do everything exactly the same as for the Venus Fly Trap, i.e. use a 13 cm half-pot, a mixture of moss–peat and sand, and stand the pot in rainwater. Keep the plant on a warm, well-lit windowsill.

How to get more
New plants will grow up from the roots now and then, so you can break these off. Otherwise, just

sprinkle seeds on the same growing medium and stand the pot in rainwater. The seeds are produced by the flowers without any help from you.

Suppliers: Sarracenia Nurseries, Marston Exotics, Peter Paul's, Plant Shops Botanical, Carnivorous Gardens, Hinode-Kadan, Millingimbi Nursery, New Dawn Nursery, Renate Parsley, Thysanotus-Seed-Mailorder, Harald Weiner

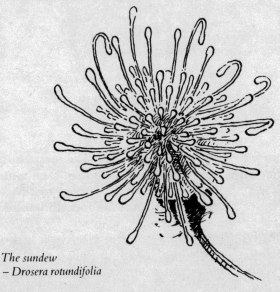

The sundew
– Drosera rotundifolia

The Dracula Plant – Sarracenia flava and
The Huntsmans Cup – Sarracenia purpurea
These are both types of pitcher plant from North America. The Dracula Plant has many common names including the Yellow Trumpet and the Tender Trap. Pitcher plants have two types of leaf. The winter leaves are long and ordinary but the

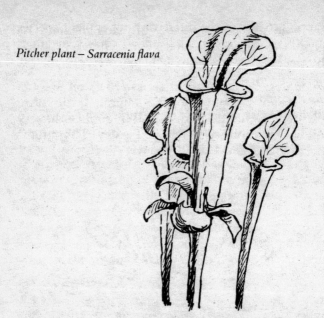

Pitcher plant – Sarracenia flava

summer ones are amazingly beautiful and specially designed to take advantage of all the flies that pass by. These special pitcher leaves are long thin tubes which are perfect stomachs, lying in wait for a fly to eat. Both S. flava and S. purpurea produce a sticky sweet liquid at the top lip of the pitcher which attracts flies, ants or other insects. The insect walks down into the tube which leads to more and more sweet food. When it tries to climb back up, it may realize what a terrible mistake it has made. There are many hairs pointing downwards and these stop the insect from escaping. If it tries to fly out it usually bumps into the roof which hangs over the trap and makes escape very difficult. The sticky liquid also makes the insect giddy and of course that does not help it either. In the end the insect falls back in and is trapped. Most of the different pitcher plant species quickly produce digestive juices, the fly or ant is slowly dissolved and the pitcher absorbs all the goodness.

How to grow
Pitcher plants, especially these two, are very easy to grow. If possible, buy mature plants. Make a mixture of two parts moss–peat and one part 'Pearlite' or 'Vermiculite'. Use a 13–16 cm full-size pot for S. flava, or a 5 cm dwarf pot for S. purpurea. Put your pitcher plant in the pot and fill with soil so that the leaves and pitchers are not covered. Now stand the pot in a tray of rainwater from spring until autumn. In winter remove the tray and only use a little water to keep the soil just damp. Leave these plants outdoors in winter.

How to get more
Every now and then, assuming all goes well, your pitcher plant will outgrow or fill its pot. If you want several plants, carefully put your hand on the soil, fingers either side of the plant and turn the pot upside down. Give the pot a sharp tap and the plant will fall out. Carefully clean or wash off the soil and you will see a part of the plant that looks like a thick stubby root with leaves growing from it. This is not a root, it is a stem that grows underground. Using a clean sharp knife you can cut the stem into several pieces about 4 cm long. Each piece will grow into a new plant and you treat each one exactly the same as the original plant.

Seeds can also be used but fresh seed is important if you are to get good results. To produce your own seeds you will need two pitcher plants and both must flower. You will have to move pollen from

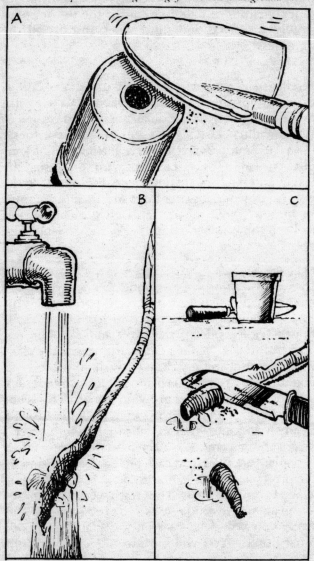

one flower on to the other, using a paintbrush or tooth-pick to collect pollen from the flower and move it on to the stigma of another flower. Then wait. If you have been successful, the seed pod will swell up after the petals die. (If the plants are out-doors, insects will do this for you.)

Collect the seed, mix it with a little damp sand in a plastic bag and put the bag in a fridge for 6–8 weeks (more if you like). In February, put the seeds on to the moss peat and sand mixture and cover it with a very thin layer. Now stand the pot in water and wait for the seeds to germinate. It will take about six weeks. Move the young plants to bigger pots when-ever they get too big for the pot they are in.

Suppliers: Sarracenia Nurseries, Marston Exotics, Peter Paul's, Plant Shops Botanical, Carnivorous Gardens, Hinode-Kadan, Millingimbi Nursery, New Dawn Nursery, Renate Parsley, Thysanotus-Seed-Mailorder, Harald Weiner

Butterworts – Pinguicula grandiflora, Pinguicula caudata

These are fairly well known as a result of their incredible ability to catch flies. Pinguicula caudata (pin-gwick-you-lar cor-dar-ta) or the Mexican Butterwort is a windowsill plant that is happy to grow indoors. Providing it gets some sunlight, it is a pretty green plant that looks very like a fat, squashed cabbage, but it has the advantage of flowering in both summer and winter. This is the best known butterwort because orchid-growers often keep it. Orchids are very rare and expensive plants. Some can be easily damaged by pests includ-ing a particular kind of fly. The orchid-growers protect their plants by growing the butterwort which kindly eats the flies!

Both butterworts stop growing insect-eating leaves in winter, and P. grandiflora forms a tight, small resting bud to protect it from winter frosts. It is an outdoor plant which can still be found in the wild in Ireland and Europe.

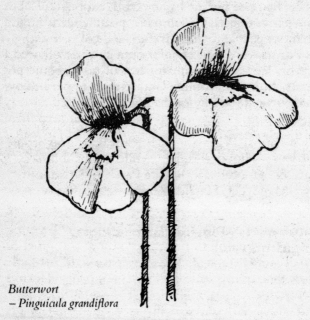

Butterwort
– Pinguicula grandiflora

How to grow

There are two main types of plants to worry about, some being hardy and the others tender. 'Hardy' means that the plants will survive frost, whereas 'tender' plants are liable to frost damage.

For hardy plants such as P. grandiflora you can create an artificial peat bog by filling a container or pond with moss peat and sand. Soak the mixture with rainwater, and plant your plants in it. Keep it wet all year. You will need a net or wire mesh to cover the bog or birds will peck the plants! If you have a rockery and there is a low area that is always moist you can dig a hole there, fill it with moss peat and sand and plant a butterwort which is, after all, a natural alpine plant. If you prefer, you can fill a pot with moss peat and sand and plant your plants in that.

For tender species like P. caudata you will need a 13 cm half-pot for up to three plants. Fill the pot with a mixture of moss-peat and silver sand. Now stand the pot in a tray of rainwater and keep the tray full all year. Put the plants in the pot and keep them in a well-lit or slightly shaded place. A windowsill is best. These plants must be kept indoors except in summer.

How to get more
Hardy varieties will propagate themselves. In January or February, carefully dig up a small resting bud and you will find it has produced a number of small buds around it. If you put these on top of some fresh soil (a peat/sand mixture), each one will form a new plant.

Tender varieties will divide into several plants during the winter. In February, you can dig up the plants and pull them apart carefully. This is called 'division'. Replant the single plants in fresh mixture. For another method you will need a few butterwort leaves. In February, dig up a plant and very carefully pull off a few of the small green leaves. Fill a small pot with some fresh, damp mixture and lay the leaves on top of it. Now put the

37

pot in a clear plastic bag and seal it with a rubber band. Place the pot in a well-lit position but not in direct sunlight. After a few weeks you will find new plants growing on the old leaves. When they are large enough you can carefully dig them up and plant them in a bigger pot. This method is called taking 'leaf cuttings'.

Suppliers: Sarracenia Nurseries, Marston Exotics, Peter Paul's, Plant Shops Botanical, Carnivorous Gardens, Hinode-Kadan, Millingimbi Nursery, New Dawn Nursery, Renate Parsley, Thysanotus-Seed-Mailorder, Harald Weiner

Bladderwort – Utricularia

Bladderworts – Utricularia
These plants are incredibly small, they eat animals and very few people grow them. This is strange

38

because they are very pretty and often easy to grow. Unfortunately you cannot see them eating very easily. Utricularia vulgaris (you-trick-you-lair-ee-ah vulgar-iss) or the Common Bladderwort is a water plant and its traps grow underwater. The traps are a bit like tiny squashed stomachs. When an animal touches a small trigger the stomach snaps open. As a result, water rushes into the trap carrying with it anything nearby, including the unlucky insect. Of course, the insect now becomes not only the dinner-guest but the dinner as well. This is the fastest movement known in plants and is almost impossible to film clearly.

Bladderworts grow in Britain as well as most other parts of the world. While U. vulgaris or U. intermedia are easiest to observe when the traps are operating, U. sandersonnii will flower non-stop for most of the year.

How to grow
U. vulgaris must have a fairly large area like a large fish-tank or pond. Fill it with rainwater and make sure that algae does not take over. In a fish-tank it is best to use shade to prevent algae forming. In a pond use water-lilies and other water plants. If you have a lot of bladderwort, some fish will help the pond to keep itself in perfect condition. If you use a tank, feed the plant with water fleas (Daphnia) in summer. In winter, the plant will rest in a tight bud.

U. sandersonii should be planted indoors in equal amounts of moss-peat and sand. The pot should be stood in rainwater so that the water comes two-thirds of the way up the pot. You can keep it like this in bright sun or on a windowsill all year. If your plant is healthy it will spread and flower very quickly. Replant every year in a fresh mixture. The traps are too small to see, but the flowers, hundreds of them, attract attention even though they are very small.

Suppliers: Marston Exotics, Sarracenia Nurseries, Peter Paul's, Plant Shops Botanical, Carnivorous Gardens, Hinode-Kadan, Millingimbi Nursery, New Dawn Nursery, Renate Parsley, Thysanotus-Seed-Mailorder, Harald Weiner

The Cobra Lily – Darlingtonia californica
Of all the carnivorous plants in the world surely this must be one of the most striking. As the name suggests, Darlingtonia californica (darling-tone-ee-ah cal-lee-four-nee-cah) looks almost exactly like a cobra snake about to strike.

The Cobra Lily is a type of pitcher plant closely related to the Sarracenias. Flies enter the trap through a small hole underneath the hood of the pitcher. Once they are inside, the flies are fooled into trying to get out by flying in any direction except the correct one. Eventually, exhausted, they fall to the bottom of the trap where digestive juices slowly turn them into yet another tasty meal.

The pitchers are not only striking, they are also very attractive. The flowers too are fascinating, lantern-like objects held high above the plant and coloured in beautiful shades of red. Few people could fail to be amazed and impressed by the Cobra Lily.

How to grow
Use a soil made up of a mixture of moss-peat and sphagnum moss in equal amounts or use plain sphagnum moss with no peat at all (this is better) in

a 13 cm half-pot. Stand the pot in rainwater or distilled water in the spring, summer and autumn but, during the winter, when growth stops temporarily, keep the soil just moist. Darlingtonia is quite happy in full sun or partial shade. It is fully hardy so it can be grown outdoors all the year round or in an unheated greenhouse.

How to get more
As your plant grows older you will find new plants appear, especially near the edge of the pot. Carefully dig these up and cut them from the parent plant, leaving at least 2–3 cm of root attached to the new plant. You can then replant it in a new pot and treat it in the same way as the parent. If you do get seeds, these should be sown immediately. Use a mixture of peat and sand, kept moist, with the seeds on the surface of the soil and a plastic bag over the pot. This should be kept in a well-lit place but out of direct sunlight. If the seeds germinate they can be planted in pure sphagnum moss when they are big enough to move easily.

Suppliers: Sarracenia Nurseries, Marston Exotics, Peter Paul's, Plant Shops Botanical, Carnivorous Gardens, Hinode-Kadan, Millingimbi Nursery, New Dawn Nursery, Renate Parsley, Thysanotus-Seed-Mailorder, Harald Weiner

3   Exploding plants

There is nothing as dramatic as a plant that explodes into flame. Dictamnus – the Burning Bush – is one of the most theatrical plants in nature.

Many plants have seed pods which explode. This is a fairly normal method by which plants spread their seeds. Seed spreading or dispersal is interesting and there are all sorts of methods used by plants. Some seeds fly, either using wings like the sycamore seed or using parachutes like the dandelion. Seeds can be shaken out of a pod like a baby's rattle such as in poppies, while other seeds, including burrs, can grab hold of passing animals and then fall off later. Another clever method is having seeds that are pretty enough to make you want to eat them like tomatoes. Tomato seeds go in one end of you and straight out of the other end! Tomato plants often flourish in sewage farms.

However, the most impressive method of dispersal is by a plant which spreads its seeds by using explosions. Not only do they work very efficiently for the plant but they are also great fun. There are many examples but some are better than others.

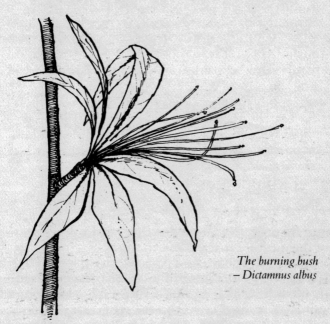

The burning bush – Dictamnus albus

The Burning Bush – Dictamnus fraxinella, Dictamnus albus

Be careful with this one. The first danger is fire and so you must make sure you don't do anything to cause damage to people, animals or property. The other danger is being misled into buying the wrong plant. Many plants have the name 'Burning Bush' but only Dictamnus catches fire.

On a hot day, with no wind at all, striking a match near this plant would cause it to burst into flames. Actually, Dictamnus does not really want to catch fire. It happens to have leaves which are full of a fragrant oil. Fragrant oils always boil at a very low temperature and most oils burn. In strong sun this oil turns to gas (or boils) and is ready and easy to burn. If a flame just happens to pass by, the bush will catch fire. Luckily, flames do not usually pass bushes very often, so not many plants explode into flame. Another name for Dictamnus is the Gas Plant and you can see why.

Happily the plant does not get burnt even if the oil does catch fire. The living plant not only looks nice but also smells nice, so do not set fire to your bush on purpose. If you must experiment with it, be sure to ask an adult to help you.

How to grow
Dictamnus is an outdoor plant. Plant in ordinary soil and do not keep it too wet. A little sand in the soil will help.

How to get more
The easiest way is probably by root cuttings. Dig up a plant in March or April. Find a fat, healthy root and cut it off. Now chop the root into 3 cm long pieces. Plant these in a pot in moist, sandy soil covered by 5 cm more soil. Keep it moist and put the pot in a greenhouse or indoors until after June. When the new plants that appear are big enough or in October, whichever comes first, plant them in the garden.

You can plant seeds just under the soil surface in August or September. The weather will do everything else.

Suppliers: Beth Chatto

Touch–Me–Not – Impatiens noli–me–tangere

This plant is best known as Busy Lizzy and all of them (there are many kinds) are quite easy to grow. As the seed pod gets riper, it gets ready to burst. Eventually it is so ripe that absolutely any change will set it off – a change in the wind, a change in the temperature, or even rain will be enough. As the plant's name suggests (it means 'do not touch me'), it will explode if you touch it. Try touching the pods every day until they are ripe. Perhaps you should wear sunglasses so that seeds cannot accidentally get into your eyes.

How to grow
The main problem with this plant is not so much how to grow it as how not to grow it. It is one of those plants known to be invasive, which means it spreads very quickly whether you want it to or not. It is so easy to grow from seed that all you need do is sprinkle them on the soil wherever you want them to grow. You can do this in April. Plant the seeds outside in ordinary soil. They should be just under the surface in a place that will get plenty of sun. When the young plants are about 2–3 cm high, take out enough (especially the smaller ones) so that the ones you leave are all about 10–15 cm apart. If you grow the plants in pots they like plenty of water.

How to get more
To grow more, collect the seeds and plant them

next year. Your plant will manage this by itself anyway.

If you grow a plant with particularly nice features, say a beautiful flower colour or leaves with a yellow edge, it may be that you want more of this type. Seeds will produce plants that look like the parent but may not be exact copies. To get an exact copy or 'clone' you must take cuttings. Find the end of a branch of the plant and cut it off so it is at least 7 cm long. If it is longer cut it into 7 cm long pieces each one of which is called a cutting. Dip the bottom cut end of each piece into some water, shake the piece once and then dip it into a little rooting hormone. You can buy this in any good garden centre but be very careful never to get any of the powder on your hands. If it does, you must wash it off immediately. Tap the cutting so that the excess rooting hormone falls off.

Mix some soil consisting of equal amounts of peat and sand. Fill a 7 cm pot with the soil and stand it in water for 10–15 minutes. Then let it drain for another 15 minutes. Now make four holes with a pencil in the soil of each pot far apart from each other at the edge of the pot. Put 3 cm of the powdered end of a cutting in each hole and press the soil gently to close up the hole. Finally, cover the pot and plants with a clear or opaque plastic bag, blow it up gently (just like a balloon) and seal it with a rubber band or wire tie. Place it somewhere bright and warm but not in direct sunlight. In five weeks you will be able to open the bag, gently knock out the cuttings and find a beautiful new set of roots. You can plant these outdoors in the ground or individually in pots.

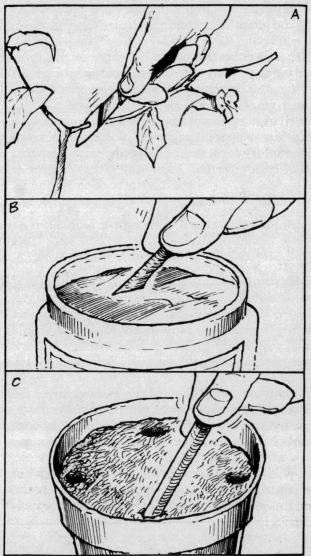

Suppliers: Chiltern Seeds, Thompson and Morgan and most good seed suppliers. Plants often available at nurseries in summer

Ruellia tuberosa

A fantastic plant. If you can get the seed try dropping one in a glass of water. Not much happens until all of a sudden, BANG!!, it explodes.

This is not a common plant in this country and not many people have heard of it. In India, where it comes from, it is just a weed. All the same, the flowers are pretty.

How to grow

This plant likes to be nice and warm, 21°C (70°F) or more all year round, although it will survive if a little colder on occasions. It must be kept indoors and prefers a soil made up from loam, leaf mould, peat and sand, all in equal amounts. You can use John Innis No. 2 Potting Compost mixed with some sand instead. Stand the pot in water until the surface of the soil is damp. Then drain it and only water again when the soil begins to feel dry or if the leaves begin to droop.

How to get more

What fun! To get more plants you can use seed. To get seeds you must open up the seed pods, and to do that you drop them in water. 3 – 2 – 1 – take cover – BANG! There it goes again. What a pity it is such a hard plant to find.

When you do have seeds, plant them in the John Innis and sand mixture. Stand the pot in water for ten minutes. Now let it drain for ten minutes. Put the pot in a clear plastic bag, seal the top and place it in a light, warm place 21–23°C (70–75°F). Seeds should begin to germinate in a few weeks. When they are big enough, open the bag a little. Gradually open it more each day until you can remove the pot altogether. Then prick out the small plants and put them into separate pots.

Suppliers: Chiltern Seeds, but do be patient – they cannot always be supplied. It is well worth persevering until you get some

Rock rose – Cistus purpureus

Rock Rose – Cistus

Although this plant is sometimes called Rock Rose, it is normally known as Cistus (sis-tuss). It is a plant that does not like too much water and hates wind, so give it some shelter. Once again, the seed pods

49

explode, but Cistus has so many pods that lots of them are bursting at almost the same time. If you stand near it and keep quiet, you will hear it crackling whenever the pods are ripe and the weather is warm.

How to grow
Plant outdoors in light, well-drained soil. (Add peat and sand to the soil if it looks muddy or sticky.) Plant near a wall to shelter the plant from the wind. The plants like rock gardens.

How to get more
Plant seeds in sandy soil in a cold greenhouse or outside under glass. Do this in March. When plants are about 2–3 cm high, you can move them into pots. In June the plants can be taken outside and put in their favourite place. Cuttings can also be taken in September. Cut off the end of a branch so that it is 10 cm long. Pull off the leaves at the bottom for about 2–3 cm. If possible, dip the bare end in a little rooting powder, but be very careful not to get the powder on your hands. Fill a pot with sandy soil. Make a thin hole with a pencil 2–3 cm deep in the soil and put the bare end of the cutting in it. Keep the cuttings in their pots inside a cold greenhouse or under glass until next June and keep the soil just slightly damp all the time. Then plant them in the garden.

Suppliers: Sandwich Nurseries. Good garden centres should be able to supply several varieties of plant

4 Followers of the sun

Some plants move so quickly they have become curiosities such as the Venus Fly Trap and Sensitive Mimosa. Others move so slowly you would need to sit for hours before you noticed any movement. Between these two extremes are those plants which move just fast enough to be seen and of that group, sun-worshippers are an example.

Most plants move with the sun, following it so that they can receive the light. In this way they use the light, water and carbon dioxide (which we breathe out) to make their own food. This process is known as photosynthesis.

Leaves, in fact any green part of a plant, make food, but flowers do not so why do they follow the sun? To answer this we must look at the contents of a flower. A male flower contains stamens which make pollen. A female flower contains a pistol which makes ovules. (Some flowers are both male and female so they have stamens and pistols.) If a pollen grain successfully joins with an ovule the result is a seed which will grow into a new plant, but before this happens the pollen and ovules must be ripe. This happens as the flower grows and the sun helps to dry off the pollen when it is ripe.

At this stage the coloured flowers will want insects to visit them so that pollen can be carried from one flower to another. If the flower is open it is also much bigger so that as much light as possible will be reflected from it. This helps the insects to see it, and this means that some flowers not only turn to face the sun, but also open when the sun is out.

The plants that follow are more beautiful and less

common than many of those found in ordinary shops and garden centres. You can choose plants that are a little different by writing to a specialist.

The Tulip – Tulipa kaufmanniana ancilla

This tulip is a lovely plant and grows only 12 cm tall. The flowers are white with a red rim. They look beautiful in a small pot, about five in a 15 cm pot, or in a small group in the garden. They flower in February or perhaps March and then you can experiment. When the flowers are open, try moving the plant into the shade, or if it is planted in the garden cover the plant with a dark cover like a large flower-pot. See how long it takes for the flower to close. If you bring back the light does the flower open up again?

The tulip
– Tulipa kaufmanniana ancilla

How to grow
Use a good soil or potting compost with a little sand

in it so that it will not be water-logged. Tulips like alkaline soil so if yours is acid you can add a little lime. Do not get lime on your body as it will burn. Put five bulbs in a 15 cm pot or plant about 2 cm apart in the ground. The bulbs should be covered by about 2 cm of soil. If in a pot, water once in December and once in January. When you begin to see leaves, place the pot in full sunlight and you can water it regularly so the soil is always damp. After flowering, continue to water, and once or twice a month add some fertilizer (bought from any good garden centre). When the leaves begin to turn yellow, water less and less. Finally, when the leaves are all dead, stop watering and leave until next December. You can dig up the bulbs and store them dry, in a paper bag in the dark.

How to get more
Seeds take a very long time to grow, so it is probably best to use 'offsets'. These are baby bulbs which grow on the side of the parent. After the leaves are dead you can carefully dig up the bulbs. Any offsets can be carefully broken off and treated like the rest. To get extra offsets, you must cut off the flowers as soon as possible!

Suppliers: Avon Bulbs (or any other bulb specialist). Do try dwarf tulips (13 cm or shorter)

The Telegraph Plant – Desmodium gyrans
An interesting plant which originates in India, the Telegraph Plant is fairly attractive, and a moving plant that is surprisingly rarely seen. It grows to about 1 m in height, has violet flowers and is of interest because of its leaves.

'Telegraph' means to signal over a distance and

the leaves certainly do seem to signal. They spend the whole day moving to follow the sun so that they can capture as much light as possible. In the wild, Desmodium gyrans (dez-mode-ee-um jire-ans) is often found growing beneath taller shrubs and trees so it needs as much light as possible. No matter where the sun moves to, the leaves always change position so that they face it. Try placing a bright light by the side of a plant and see if you can cause the leaves to move.

It is difficult to obtain this plant unless you buy seeds.

The telegraph plant
– Desmodium gyrans

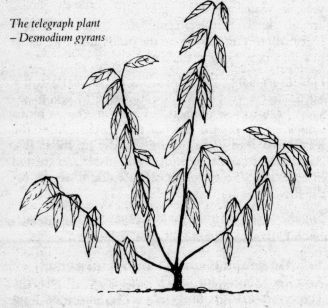

How to grow
This plant prefers a soil consisting of equal amounts of peat, loam and silver sand. If you cannot easily get these you could use John Innis No. 1 (instead of

loam) and any soil-free compost (instead of peat) and sand. These can all be purchased in small amounts from most shops that have a plant section.

Use plenty of water, preferably rain or soft water, for most of the year. Only use enough to keep the soil damp during winter. The summer temperature should be 18–23°C (65–75°F), and the winter, 12–18°C (55–65°F). The leaves die down completely in winter.

How to get more
Sow seeds in sandy soil (equal peat and sand) at 23–26°C (75–80°F) in February or March. For cuttings, in March or April, cut off 6–8 cm lengths of the plant, dip the cut end in rooting hormone and insert it into a pot of sandy soil. Water the soil, allow it to drain, cover the pot and plant with a plastic bag and leave for a few weeks. New roots should be well established after about five weeks and you can then treat the plant as an adult.

Suppliers: Chiltern Seeds, Thompson and Morgan

The Sensitive Plant (Sensitive Mimosa) – Mimosa pudica

A very peculiar plant to all who see or know of it, Mimosa pudica (mim-oh-sir pew-dee-cah) is a delicate and attractive plant with feather-shaped leaves. When in flower, it can be covered by many little balls of pink, purple or rose, but the ability of the leaves to move rapidly is of most interest. Every night, Mimosa will go to sleep with opposite pairs of leaves closing together. The whole plant ends up looking ragged, as if it is either very unhealthy or dying. However, in the day, although the leaves open to receive sunlight, they will close very quickly if stimulated. Tap the plant or leaves and they shut almost immediately.

This is a clever adaptation to protect the plant from damage. If an animal attempts to eat Mimosa, the leaves close when touched and the plant looks ill. Now the animal has a choice of continuing to eat the 'sick' Mimosa or choosing another nice, healthy plant nearby. They usually choose to eat another plant and so Mimosa survives.

If you have more than one plant, it is worth experimenting with a burning incense stick. Light the stick and then blow out the flame. The end will continue to burn, giving off smoke and a smell that is meant to be attractive. Take the stick and deliberately burn the very end of one leaf. As soon as it

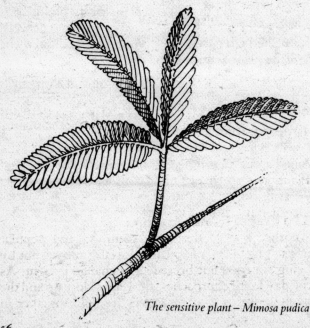

The sensitive plant – Mimosa pudica

moves, stop burning it. Only one or two leaves will drop. Now try again but this time when the leaf drops keep burning it. You will see that the leaves next to it drop. The longer you burn Mimosa the more leaves drop.

Another point of interest is that medicines or drugs which make people feel less pain also slow down or stop the movement in Mimosa.

How to grow

Mimosa will grow well in any well-lit, warm place. Keep the temperature at 18–23°C (65–75°F). Use a pot that is between 9–13 cm wide, and commercial potting compost. Alternatively, mix equal amounts of peat, sand and loam. Water the plant by standing the pot in its own depth of water for 5–10 minutes. Then let it drain. Water again when the soil feels dry. If possible spray with water too as Mimosa enjoys humidity but it will survive without it.

How to get more

Plant seeds in spring. Just cover them with soil, stand the pot in water for five minutes and then drain. Finally, cover with a plastic bag until the seeds germinate, then treat exactly like a mature plant.

Suppliers: Chiltern Seeds, Thompson and Morgan. Plants are available at good garden centres.

The Prayer Plant – Maranta

Another one of the more common and popular house plants, Maranta (mer-ant-ah), moves not by being touched but because of a change in light. As the day's end approaches, the leaves close up and the plant looks as if all its leaves are held together in prayer. Again, this is probably to protect the plant from being eaten. At night, the leaves cannot use sunlight to make food so they need not lie flat in an attempt to collect light. By folding up, they make the plant less obvious and therefore less attractive to any wandering nocturnal animals that might fancy a quick bite.

Not surprisingly, as Marantas are already popular, they are very attractive. The leaves are very strikingly patterned and there are obvious differences between species. As there are so many species it is possible to start a collection of them.

*The prayer plant
– Maranta leuconeura*

How to grow
Use a commercial potting compost or two parts peat, one part loam and one part sand. The pot

should be about 3 cm wider than the clump of leaves. Marantas dislike cold so keep them away from cold windows. In temperate climates they must be kept indoors in winter. Keep the soil moist all the time, using rain or distilled water if at all possible. The leaves also enjoy being sprayed. These plants adore well-lit places even though they will survive in dim corners. The leaves will only move if you keep the plant in the light. However, do not grow your plant in direct sunlight or the leaves will burn. Repot the plant each year.

How to get more
When you repot the plant, just take a knife and carefully cut the clump in half. Any small, rooted pieces can be used.

Suppliers: Plant Shops Botanical. Any florist or garden centre should be able to supply several species

5   The great pretenders

Surely one of the strangest things a plant can do is pretend to be something else. There are different reasons for doing this and all sorts of things can be copied, including other plants, animals and even rocks.

The Bee Orchid – Ophrys apifera

Ophrys apifera (off-riss ape-if-err-ah) looks like a bumble bee. The flower has evolved especially to look like a female bee. The male bee is attracted to what it thinks is a female and while visiting the plant helps to pollinate it by delivering pollen from another plant and collecting pollen from this plant. In exchange for this favour the bee does not get anything at all!

The Bee Orchid used to be quite common in England but unfortunately it has been allowed to die out. This is true of many plants, but it is very obvious with orchids, almost all of which are now rare or no longer found in Britain. Modern farming methods and building are mainly responsible but so are plant collectors who steal them from the countryside. They are fairly expensive but easier to buy than to find. Do go out into the countryside to look for orchids; they are beautiful to see in the wild. However, DO NOT dig up wild orchids (or any other wild plants). Not only is it illegal it is also unnecessary. You will get healthier plants from good nurseries and the wild plants should be left where everyone can enjoy them.

How to grow
Plant outdoors or in a cold greenhouse. Use a good

soil with a lot of sand to help drain off extra water. Bee Orchids also enjoy lime, so add chalk, which is best done by adding old mortar rubble. (A mixture of old brick and the cement used to stick them, well broken and mixed with soil and sand will be very good.) You can give lots of water when the plant is growing, but stop watering when the leaves go yellow and die off in autumn. You can start again in spring. Bee Orchids love the sun. O. insectifera, the Fly Orchid, is another orchid you can grow in the same way. There are also other Mediterranean members of the Ophrys family that are easy to obtain but they need a greenhouse in which to grow.

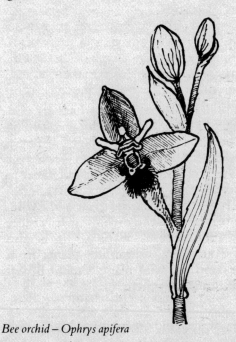

Bee orchid – Ophrys apifera

How to get more
If you can find a cheap, easy way to get more plants you are an excellent gardener. Propagating usually takes a very long time or a lot of money. If you really do get interested in them, orchids are so popular there are many books that will teach you how to grow them from seed, although it is complicated, time-consuming and expensive.

Suppliers: Avon Bulbs. (Overseas orders will require an import permit as this is an orchid. Contact your Government Dept of Plant Health before ordering this or any orchid)

Living Stones – Lithops

I think everybody would have to agree that these plants are among the most amazing in the world. Most people think of them as a type of cactus but they do not have any spikes. In fact, they do not have a lot of anything. The whole plant consists of some root with just two leaves. Each year the old leaves die as two new ones replace them. You can also look forward to a beautiful daisy-like flower if you take good care of the plant.

However, the best part of the plant is that the leaves look exactly like stones and for a very good reason. Lithops live in a very dry desert in South Africa. Any animal living in the desert is bound to appreciate a free drink and the animals do not mind if they eat just to quench their thirst. The Lithops plants probably started life with a fairly ordinary appearance but one or two looked a bit like stones. The ordinary ones would get eaten more often, leaving the stone ones because they were harder to find. Gradually, only the plant that looked like

Living stones – Lithops

stones survived, which is why they are called Living Stones.

How to grow

Lithops like plenty of light all year. A south-facing windowsill is essential if you do not have a greenhouse, but they are so small and attractive they will be a welcome addition to a window display. Water them carefully from May until October. From November until the end of April, do not water them at all. You can let them get quite cool in winter, though no lower than −7°C (45°F), but in summer keep them at 15°C (60°F) or hotter. For soil, use a commercial cactus soil or make your own. To do this, take some brick dust and add an equal amount of mortar rubble. To this mixture add an equal amount of loam. To that mixture add an equal amount of sharp sand. What a performance! It is much easier to buy cactus soil.

How to get more
You can buy seed but to get your own you will need to wait until the plants flower. Then 'tickle' the flowers with a paint-brush. If a small seed pod forms when the flower dies, then you will get seeds, but they are very difficult to collect as they are so tiny.

Sow the seeds on special, fresh, damp cactus soil in a seed tray covered with a glass or plastic top. Do not water for a whole year and keep the plants warm, about 20°C (68°F). Do not allow direct sunlight on them but keep them in good light.

After a year, you can move them to pots using a toothpick to carefully dig them up, but only move them when you have to. After the first year grow them like the adult plants.

Suppliers: **Abbeybrook**

6 Plants that live on air

Would you believe it? There are some plants that do not grow in any soil at all and their roots can just hang in the air. There are even some that actually grow on telephone wires.

Air Plants – Tillandsia

If you had been able to visit a friend's greenhouse or conservatory during the Victorian era, you might have been lucky to see a collection of really bizarre plants. They are the Air Plants or Tillandsia (till-and-see-ah) found in tropical and sub-tropical America. Unfortunately, because they all come from Central and South America, all of them were grown under tropical conditions. When Europe was at war, many greenhouses were destroyed by bombs or the plants died through lack of attention. Some collections were simply thrown away or died as they were removed to make way in the greenhouse for food such as tomatoes. Luckily there were a few people who were interested enough to keep collecting the plants and now there are Air Plants on sale in most areas.

It is very difficult to describe just one as there are so many different types, but they all have one thing in common. They have almost no roots. In the wild, the plants usually use their small roots to hold tight on to branches of trees. Other plants have large roots so that they can get water, but Air Plants have no need to worry. They get all the water they want by 'sucking' it out of the air through their leaves. The leaves are specially adapted to do this and in really hot, humid jungles they never need to actually be watered as there is so much water in the air. If you have a tropical greenhouse you may not

Air plant – Tillandsia

need to water your Air Plants but you can grow them without a greenhouse with the occasional spray of water.

Some Air Plants are interesting in another way. In the wild, they have a strange relationship with ants. The plant is able to let the ants live inside it in air spaces that appear to have been specially designed as ant homes. The ants are quite fierce little creatures and plant collectors have had a nasty surprise when their hand is suddenly covered in lots of little ants all taking rather nasty bites. The ants gain the advantage of a home, and the plant gains the advantage of protection from plant-eating animals. This relationship between two different types of living things where both of them profit from the other has a special name – symbiosis (sim-by-oh-sis).

Finally, you might like to know that Air Plants are relatives of the pineapple.

T. butzii – Possibly the most attractive Air Plant. The plant has a wide, bulb-shaped base with long, thin leaves looking almost like snakes coming out of the top and curling down. The dark green leaves are blotched with black, giving a final touch to the strange appearance. This Air Plant is one of the species which provides a home for ants in the wild. One of the easiest to grow.

T. streptophylla – This plant has long leaves that are about 2.5 cm wide. They curl all over the place when kept properly making this fairly large plant look quite spectacular.

T. argentea – Completely different from the two above, this looks almost like a collection of soft cactus spines stuck together. The leaves are long, thin and covered in white hairs. When dry, the plant is a whitish grey but when sprayed it changes to a beautiful green.

T. caput-medusae – Another of the Air Plants that looks spectacularly like a collection of snakes.

T. ionantha – Very easy to grow, very small and very cheap to buy. This is one of the smallest of the common Air Plants which will fit into anyone's home. Normally just a nice shade of green but just before it flowers the middle leaves turn to red, creating a lovely appearance.

Others recommended for beginners are T. juncea, T. plumosa, T. utriculata and T. xerographica.

How to grow

As a beginner, the easiest way to grow these plants is indoors in a room that gets quite cool in the winter. You will need to plant your Air Plant on something. A nice piece of old wood or bark will look most natural. Coral or sea shells, even though they are not as natural, can give a good-looking result. (Some of the plants for sale will already be planted on a piece of wood, coral or shell.)

Tie the plant on to its new home with a piece of string. Now stick the roots of the plant to the holder with some silicone rubber glue. Do not use more glue than you have to. After twenty-four hours or more remove the string. If you have done a good job the plant will not fall off. Now put the plant where it will get plenty of light but do not allow it to get too much direct sunlight. In winter, if the room is warm, spray the plant with rainwater about once every one or two weeks. If the room is very cold spray it less, about once every month or six weeks.

Almost all the Air Plants will survive temperatures as low as or below freezing point as long as they are indoors (or in a greenhouse) and not over-watered. In the warmer months, give more water until, in summer, the plants should be sprayed once a day. It will not matter if you forget to water them, but do not let them go thirsty for too long. For perfect results, once a month, in summer, spray with a foliar feed. Any garden centre will help you choose one and the instructions will be on the packet. Finally, if rainwater is not available, you can use tap water, but it will stain your plant white after a while. If you do not have a spray just get a bucket of water and dip the whole plant in it for a few minutes.

How to get more

This is a job for experts. It is possible to grow Air Plants from seed but it takes a long time (years) and is not easy for a beginner. When you have grown Air Plants for a few years, use one of the recommended books to find out how to grow the seed. The only other way to increase your plants is from offsets. These are the new plants that grow from the side of your old plant if the conditions are right. Air Plants (and all of their relatives) flower only once in their life and then die. After flowering and some-times before, the new small plants or offsets will grow up from the side. If you are lucky you will get two or more offsets from each plant. They look best if left alone, but you can gently cut the offsets off the parent plant and plant them in a new home.

Suppliers: Vesutor, Plant Shops Botanical

The Voodoo Lily – Sauromatum guttatum (Arum caudatum)

You have to try growing one of these. Like most of the unusual plants the name was probably invented by people who wanted to sell the plant, and it has not got anything at all to do with Voodoo. It will flower on a windowsill with no soil, no food, no water and no attention. It really does seem to live on air. In fact all the food and water it needs is in the plant already when you buy it and you will need to plant it in a pot after it has flowered. Sauromatum guttatum (sore-oh-mart-um goo-tart-um) or Arum caudatum (ah-rum cor-dart-um) is an aroid so you will finds its flower is as peculiar as that of Arum maculatum or Dracunculus. Unfortunately, this plant is nearly always wrongly named. It really is Sauromatum and not an Arum. Good plant specialists will name it correctly, but garden centres and shops with plant counters love to sell this plant with the wrong name.

How to grow
Buy it, put it on a windowsill and forget about it. After it has flowered, plant it in a pot or in the garden. Use a well-drained soil made by adding sand to any soil you have. If you plant it in the garden you need do nothing else. In a pot, you should keep the soil damp but not wet throughout the year. The plant should be buried about 9 cm deep.

How to get more
In a pot or garden the plant will divide regularly by itself. If you see you have more than one plant you can dig it up, when it is not in flower, and cut off the new small plants from the parent. If you do this in winter, you can grow the larger plants on the windowsill.

Suppliers: Avon Bulbs. These are also often sold in garden shops as novelty plants

7 Parasites: plants that need other plants

Millions of years ago, the plant kingdom was already very well established. Long before animals appeared, plants had managed to find ways of surviving in the sea, rivers, lakes and on land.

There were many problems facing the plants, one of which was how to obtain food and at first there were probably two ways. One was to make food using sunlight, carbon dioxide gas and water, the method used by all green plants and called photosynthesis. Plants that could not make their own food probably used rotting plants to provide food and absorbed the goodness released from them.

It is assumed that all life is designed to reproduce itself and everything else a living organism does should simply help reproduction. If this is true then flowers are the most important part of a flowering plant as they produce the seeds for reproduction. The trouble is that the flowers still need food to produce the seeds and so, after millions of years of experimenting, some plants managed to find a way of concentrating their energy on using flowers to reproduce while stealing food from other plants. There are many such plants, some using flowers for reproduction and some using other methods, but they all share the same characteristic – that of stealing food from other plants. They are parasites, the Draculas of the plant world, which live by sucking the goodness out of a poor defenceless host.

Ivy Broomrape – Orobanche hederae

Almost all of the parasitic plants are specialists that need to find a particular type of plant, or host, to feed on. There are several Broomrapes, but this one, Orbanche hederae (orrow-ban-chee head-err-ay), needs ivy. If it finds some, it grows inside the ivy and uses any food it can get to survive. For most of the year you cannot even see the Broomrape, but it is there, waiting. Just once a year the Broomrape flowers. This is the only time you can see it but it is well worth the wait as the flowers are both strange and attractive.

How to grow

Get some wild ivy with nice healthy roots from a garden. You can either pull up a piece or just dig out the soil so you can see the roots. Now you must plant the seeds of the Broomrape so that they can touch the ivy roots. Make the ivy roots wet, and sprinkle the seed on to the wet ivy roots. Then cover the roots with soil. If the ivy is in a pot, put it outdoors. Water it well and keep the plant moist if it is in a pot; otherwise it will look after itself. If you are successful it should flower after several years.

One important thing. Plant Broomrape seeds as soon as you get them or they will die.

How to get more
If your plants flower, you may be able to collect seed from the seed pods but otherwise you will not be able to get more plants. This plant can take anything up to five years to flower, so you really will need lots of patience. Remember, until it flowers you cannot even tell if it is growing!

Suppliers: Chiltern Seeds

The Indian Paint Brush – Castilleja rhexifolia

This is an example of a plant that is partway between being able to feed itself and being a parasite. It has all the 'normal' plant parts, but it just is not good enough at making its own food to survive. It will last two or three years without a host, but to keep it for longer it requires grass.

Compared with Broomrape, this is a much easier plant to grow, and most of the year it is easy to see and quite beautiful. The stunning flowers give the plant its name as they look exactly as if they have been dipped in paint.

How to grow
Mix two parts of peat to one part of a mixture of loam, leaf mould and sand. Add some chopped, fresh turf (living grass) to act as the host. Plant outside in a garden if possible, or a pot, but try not to let it dry out too much. If in a pot, change the soil every two or three years.

How to get more
The plant should seed by itself, but you can collect the seed from ripe pods and plant them the next year.

Suppliers: Chiltern Seeds

8 Unusual plants to eat and drink

There are many edible plants but not all of them are as interesting to grow as the Japanese Raisin Tree or the Ground Nut. Then there are microscopic plants that are difficult or impossible to see, but can be used to make delicious drinks like Ginger Beer. It is worthwhile experimenting with these plants – after all, you never know when you may be hungry or thirsty!

The Japanese Raisin Tree – Hovenia dulcis

Fruit is a word which everyone knows but most people do not understand. For example, if you were asked to name three fruits you like to eat, you would probably say apple, orange and banana. However, apples are not fruits, at least not to a biologist or horticulturalist (somebody who studies how plants grow). The true fruit of any plant consists of a swollen ovary, the part of a flower found inside the ring of petals.

Cut an apple in half. You will see pips surrounded by a whitish green pulp and then there is a ring of fibre. The fibre and inner pulp are the ovary which has swollen slightly after the pips began to ripen. Most people throw away the swollen ovary and ovary wall which is called the apple core. So what do we eat? The nice juicy pulp is actually the swollen flower stalk and that is why it is not a fruit, it is a false fruit. Many so-called fruits are really false fruits, but the Japanese Raisin Tree is one you will not buy at your supermarket or local food shop.

Just to confuse you, this plant does not grow raisins (dried grapes). It does have lovely leaves and whitish green flowers. After the flowers die, the flower stalks swell like apples but not as big. You can pick these stalks and eat them as they are sweet and tasty – Hovenia dulcis (hoe-veen-ee-ah dull-sis) means 'sweet Hovenia'.

How to grow
Plant seeds in ordinary seed compost such as John Innis No. 1. When they have grown big enough to move (1–2 cm tall), pot them in ordinary potting compost. Keep the soil moist but not wet and allow plenty of light and air. Keep indoors or in a greenhouse and if necessary bring indoors for winter unless you can keep temperatures about 10°C (50°F).

How to get more
Seeds are best and reasonably easy to grow. If you

have several plants you can try cutting off a small length of plant. Pull off the bottom leaves to leave about four or six. Now push the 2–3 cm length of bare stem into a hole in a pot of potting compost. Fill the hole, water the plant and leave to drain. Cover the plant and pot with a plastic bag and leave in a warm, well-lit place. After two months, if you are successful, the cutting will have rooted to make a new plant. You can now treat it like a mature plant.

Suppliers: Chiltern Seeds

Ground Nut – Arachis hypogaea

When a flower is fertilized the seeds grow very quickly, using a lot of energy in the process. Most of this energy is stored inside the new seed to help it later when light, water and temperature are just right for growth to begin. Before it finds its way into the ground, the seed is a perfect target for animals which can use all its stored energy as food. Some plants allow for this by producing more seeds than necessary so that most can be eaten, leaving just a few. Other seeds have juicy coats which make them attractive to eat but the seeds are indigestible and go through an animal undamaged to eventually reach the ground. There are even seeds which contain (or have a coat containing) deadly poisons so that animals will not attempt to eat them.

These and other methods of defence are all very successful but there is, of course, another answer to the problem of stopping animals eating your seeds – why not hide them like the Ground Nut.

Also known as 'Monkey Nut', 'Peanut' and 'Earthnut', the Ground Nut is a nice example of a plant which hides its seeds. As soon as the seeds begin to develop the seed pods grow longer and longer until eventually they reach the ground. Then, as they continue to grow, the pods are forced into the ground. This hides the seeds by burying them underground where they are ready to grow. Now Ground Nuts are grown on farms to supply the world demand for peanuts. They have great value as a food because of all the energy they contain in stored fat (Ground Nut oil) and protein. They are also very tasty which explains why they are used in the cooking of any country where Ground Nuts grow naturally. They can be found served as anything from peanut butter and jam sandwiches in America to sate or satay sauce from Malaysia. There are even drinks made from Ground Nuts!

How to grow
As peanuts are usually sold ready roasted they are difficult to obtain alive. Usually they will come in 'Growing Kits' complete with instructions. Other good suppliers will supply instructions. In general, a commercial potting compost will do if kept moist and light. Grow the nuts in a greenhouse if possible. The plant is an annual so you will need to start again each year.

How to get more
Take seeds from your own plant or buy new ones.

Suppliers: Chiltern Seeds, Thompson and Morgan

The Ginger Beer Plant – Yeast
The green colour of plants is caused by a chemical they contain called chlorophyll (claw-oh-fill). It is used by the plant to turn sunlight, water and carbon dioxide gas into sugar which the plant uses for food.

Chlorophyll comes in two basic types, red and blue. If they are mixed, more of the red will look red, more of the blue will look blue and a roughly equal amount will look green. Plants that have chlorophyll are therefore very successful because they can use it to make their own food instead of having to catch it like animals.

Many plants do have chlorophyll but there are some plants that do not and these are called fungi. Almost everyone has seen part of a fungus because mushrooms and toadstools are common all over the world. These are large enough to see but many of the other fungi are microscopic and this includes one called yeast.

Yeast grows on the surface of fruit. It feeds off sugar and is able to get its energy by changing sugar into alcohol. This chemical change is called fermentation and is used to make wines and beers. Other drinks can also be made and a really tasty one is Ginger Beer. It is only very weakly alcoholic and can be made at home easily. If you would like to try, here is the recipe:

Ingredients
2 lemons
40 g root ginger
26 g cream of tartar
925 g loaf or cube sugar
9 litres water
13 g dried yeast

Put the yeast in a cup with a little water. Peel and squeeze the lemons and strain the juice. Put the juice and peel in a large bowl. Hit the ginger until it is bruised or squashed. Now add the ginger, cream of tartar and sugar to the bowl. Boil some of the water

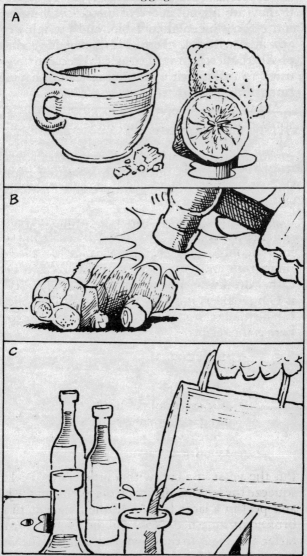

and pour it into the bowl. Leave the mixture until it is warm (though not hot). Now pour the yeast into the mixture. Stir, and cover the bowl with a large cloth. Keep it warm overnight, then use a spoon to remove the froth from the top of the liquid. Now you can drink it, but it is better to pour the liquid into bottles and seal them with corks.

DO NOT USE METAL CAPS OR SCREW TOPS. THEY ARE EXTREMELY DANGEROUS AS THEY COULD EXPLODE.

Drink the ginger beer after three days. You can change the recipe if you find it is too sweet or not sweet enough by just adding different amounts of sugar.

Suppliers: Any supermarket, home brew shop or good grocery store

9   Soap and water

At first glance, Soapwort seems to be just an ordinary-looking plant. In fact it has been cultivated by people for thousands of years, probably from the time when people lived in caves. Used with water, you could say it is the cleanest plant in the world!

If you are interested in water, you may well find ponds fascinating places to sit and watch plants and animals. You never know what might swim or float by. Of the floating plants, Duckweed is worth a closer look.

Soapwort – Saponaria

Saponaria (sap-on-air-ee-ah) was probably responsible for the creation of soap. Before soap was invented, people obviously needed to keep things clean and various plants were used as soaps. However, Saponaria is very easy and quick growing and therefore was probably widely used by primitive people.

If you grow it, you can make soap by using an old pot, water and the Soapwort. Simply cut off and wash the leaves of a plant. Chop it up into small pieces and boil them in the pot. The water will get thicker, and when you think it is thick enough you can let it cool and then use it as soap.

WARNING – as soap solution is slightly sticky do not attempt to touch it until it is completely cool and ask an adult to help you.

How to grow
Plant Saponaria outside in good garden soil. If the soil is too wet add sand. If it is too dry add peat. The plants will need no attention in the garden.

How to get more

Saponaria is easily grown from seed. Sow the seed in a seed pan of sandy soil and keep moist. The seeds should be just covered by soil. Plant the seedlings in the ground in June or July.

Suppliers: Chiltern Seeds (S. officinalis). Many garden centres specializing in herbs or rock plants will have this or other species

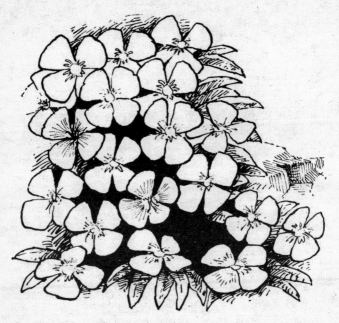

Soapwort – Saponaria 'Bressingham'

Duckweed – Lemna

If you look at any species of Lemna (lem-nah) it does not seem very exciting at all, but you would be wrong to judge it too quickly. It is a very simple floating plant consisting of one or more small leaves, perhaps 5 mm long, and some roots which dangle down in the water and can be surprisingly long.

What most people find surprising is that Duckweed is a flowering plant. It has seldom been seen in flower, but this is not surprising as this plant is a record breaker. The flowers are the smallest of any plant in the world. See if you can find any flowers during the summer months and do help yourself by using a magnifying-glass.

This plant can be used in experiments. An easy one uses one piece of Duckweed, any jam jar or small container, some water (preferably pond water), a watering-can and a bottle of liquid plant food such as 'Baby Bio'. Simply add one drop of plant food to a watering-can full of water. Use this water to half fill the jam jar and put the piece of Duckweed into the jar of water. Now leave the jar in a bright place indoors or outdoors, and see how many days it takes until there are four Duckweed leaves.

Now start again, but this time instead of using one drop of plant food use two. You can try different amounts including plain water with no food at all. What you should find is that the more food you add the faster the Duckweed grows. If you add large amounts of food, eventually it will not cause the plant to grow any faster. It is the same with you and your food. With very little food you could survive. A bit more and you might grow but not very well. More food would let you grow better, but too much would make you too big. Even more food might start to make you ill. Too much plant food would kill Duckweed.

How to grow

You would have to try very hard to kill Duckweed. All it needs is water, light and some warmth and it will grow. Place a small amount in a small container of water or a pond and there will soon be too much of it. Fortunately, some animals eat it, including ducks, so it will probably never take over completely.

How to get more

Getting more Duckweed is not a problem. Getting less is! It grows so quickly, dividing into new plants all the time that once you have a few pieces there will always be enough to give some away.

Suppliers: Stapely Water Gardens or any garden shop selling water plants. You should also be able to find Duckweed in ponds

There are some plants that have holes on purpose. If you have read about Air Plants you will have noticed that Tillandsia butzii deliberately grows holes. The hole is used as a door to 'invite' ants to use the spaces inside the plant as a home. There are many plants that have ants living with them in this way including orchids, several types of Bromeliad, many trees from the Amazon jungle, one species of tropical pitcher plant (Nepenthes bicalcarata) and some of the Eucalyptus trees of Australia.

Holes can be incredibly useful to plants if they want ants to live within them but some plants have holes for other reasons. Here are just two of them.

The Swiss Cheese Plant – Monstera deliciosa

This must be one of the most valuable plants in the world. Most people like to grow plants indoors but this usually presents major problems. Often the dull corner intended to be decorated by a living plant is hot, dry and dark, making it almost useless for growing anything. Fortunately, Monstera deliciosa (mon-steer-ah dee-liss-ee-oh-sah) is a jungle plant and can grow in very dark places. The ground it grows in naturally is always fully shaded by tall trees. Monstera does not get much light until it grows up a tree and above the jungle canopy.

The only trouble is that in a dark room the plant will never reach any bright light. Therefore it often does not grow mature leaves. In dull light the leaves grow quite far apart from each other and may look quite ordinary. In brighter light (higher up if it is in a jungle) the leaves begin to grow with deep indentations. In bright light (which would be hundreds of

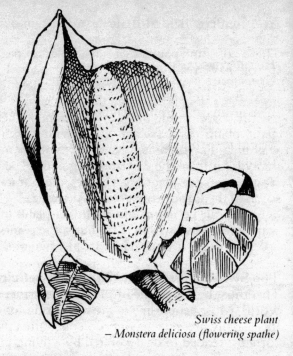

Swiss cheese plant
– Monstera deliciosa (flowering spathe)

feet up in the jungle) the leaves not only have indentations but even have holes in them. They look as if an insect has eaten bits here and there.

There are two possible reasons for the holes. As there is very little light in the jungle and because the leaves at the top will shade leaves at the bottom, it is a good idea to have holes in the top leaves. The holes act as windows and let the light through to the leaves below. Another possible reason for the holes is to do with the rain. Jungles are usually very hot. Heat and rain can easily cause plants to rot. If it did rain on the leaves and if the rain could collect in the centre of the leaf, then with the very high temperatures in the jungle the leaf could be damaged. However, with holes in the leaf, the water cannot collect and so the leaf cannot be damaged.

How to grow
Keep your plant indoors and warm. Monstera is sold as a plant suitable for deep shade. Ignore that. Use ordinary, commercial potting compost. Water the soil whenever it feels dry. Place the plant in a bright place but do not let the midday sun shine on it through glass.

How to get more
Cuttings are easy to take from Monstera. Cut off a 12 cm piece of the stem (or it can be longer). Monstera grows roots all along its stem, so you should be able to get a cutting which already has a root. Push the cutting into potting compost to a depth of about 3 cm. If there are any roots bury them as much as possible. Then treat the cutting the same as a mature plant.

Suppliers: Any indoor plant specialist or most florists

The Window Plant or Lattice Plant – Ourivandra fenestralis
This plant comes from Madagascar. It lives in rivers, which can be difficult places to survive in. The water in rivers is always rushing past the leaves, threatening to tear them apart or pull the plant away from the river bed. To avoid this, a plant can grow very long roots to hold itself firmly in the ground. It could, instead, grow very long and thin leaves or perhaps they could be feather-like. It could, of course, have very small leaves, but Ourivandra fenestralis (oo-ee-van-dra fen-ess-trar-liss) does none of these things. It simply has leaves that allow

the water to pass straight through them. Each leaf looks as if it is made of holes tied together with a little bit of leaf. It is very effective and also very beautiful.

How to grow
You will need to grow Ourivandra underwater in the warmth. If you can guarantee the temperature will always be 15°C (60°F) or more you need not heat the water. If not you can purchase a thermostat and heater from a pet or aquarium shop. You will also need an aquarium. Put 3 cm of washed gravel in the aquarium, fill it with water and either use artificial light or place the tank near a window. Buy a plant from any store that sells tropical fish as pets. Plant it by burying its roots in the gravel. If necessary tie a stone to the plant near the roots to hold it down until the roots grow.

As an aquarium with just one plant in it will look a bit strange, you could add a few other things. Why not buy any other tropical plants you like and add them as well. A few fish will also add interest, but choose ones that will not eat the plants. For colour, guppies are cheap and easy to obtain, and they are fun to watch as they breed very easily. For sheer elegance you could not do better than a few angel fish, especially if they are the 'lace' variety.

How to get more
Ourivandra will slowly spread through the gravel. When it is obvious that there are two or more plants in the gravel, dig them up and you will find they are joined together by a stem. Simply cut the stem between the plants and put them back in the gravel.

Suppliers: Any pet shop selling tropical fish though they may have to order them for you

11 Piggy-back plants

One of the most wonderful things in the world is that all living things can produce more of themselves. This is called reproduction and there are many different ways of achieving it. Sexual reproduction is very useful because it allows for the new living thing to be slightly different from all other living things, but it has the disadvantage that two living organisms are needed.

Asexual reproduction only requires one living organism. It produces two or more new living things that are all identical to the parent. Some plants and animals do this quite simply by splitting in half to make two. Others, including piggy-back plants, go through a more complicated process to produce many.

All the different methods of reproduction can be interesting, but some, like the piggy-back plants are more fun and easy to see.

Kalanchoe – Kalanchoe tubiflora, K. 'Kew Hybrid', K. jueli, K. daigremontiana

A very nice group of plants that belong to the succulents, Kalanchoe are quite closely related to cacti and have thick, fleshy leaves in which they store water. They are usually green but often have grey markings and the various species can look amazingly different. These are not really bushy plants but tend to grow straight up, sometimes as high as a metre. The flowers, and there are lots of them, can be white, yellow, orange or red, and often smell nice.

The most interesting parts are the leaves which appear to be quite ordinary at first but as the plant gets older an amazing thing happens. Little buds appear along the edges of the leaves. With time, each little bud grows into a new baby plant complete with leaves and roots and these can all be seen riding piggy-back on the old leaves. As the new plants get too heavy (or if something hits them) they fall off, hit the ground and grow where they fall. So one plant can produce thousands of new plants, all identical to each other and all of which make really good presents for friends who collect strange plants.

How to grow

Kalanchoe (cal-ann-choh) plants are quite easy to grow. They are not hardy, so you must keep them indoors in winter but any cool windowsill will be good enough. During the winter, only give the

Kalanchoe pinnata

smallest amount of water and remember to keep the plants cool. Too much water or heat will kill them.

In summer, as long as the leaves do not get wet, the plant can be watered every day and given as much light as possible. Use a commercial plant food like 'Baby Bio' once a month while the weather is good. When summer ends, cut off the top of the plant leaving only 3 cm above the soil. It may sound shocking but this will produce good, strong plants next year. Otherwise, the plants get too tall.

For soil, use a mixture of sand (or grit), peat and loam. You could use a commercial potting compost, but add an equal amount of sand or grit. Make sure that the top 2 cm of soil is ordinary fine gravel. If you cannot obtain this from a plant shop, the pet shops will sell you gravel normally used for the bottom of fish tanks.

How to get more
The easiest way is to collect a few of the baby plants from a leaf and plant them in some fresh soil. Treat them exactly like the adults. Alternatively, cut off the top of a plant in early summer. Paint the cut end with nail varnish, let it dry for a few minutes and stick the painted end into some sandy soil. Then treat it normally. Each piece should be about 7–8 cm long and stuck about 2 cm into the soil. Do not forget to add another 2 cm of gravel.

Suppliers: Barleyfield, Abbeybrook, Plant Shops Botanical

12 Everlasting plants

'Everlasting' has to be one of the most misleading words used in connection with plants because although it implies the plants never die, of course, they do.

They get their name because, if the flower stems are dried properly, they can be kept for many years and make very useful decorations. They have been used to great advantage by flower-arrangers, garden societies, florists and thousands of amateurs, but one country has managed to make flower-arranging an acceptable art all over the world.

The Japanese are experts in all aspects of gardening. They have become specialists in many different ways with marvellous collections of alpines, carnivorous plants, irises and of course the miniatures or 'Bonsais'. They call the art of flower-arranging 'Ikebana' and it relies heavily on everlasting flowers. In Japan, the arrangements are an example of beauty with simplicity, never using too many plants and always looking easy to copy. It actually needs years of practice and the gift of artistry.

To dry an Everlasting properly, you must first let it grow until the correct moment. With dried flowers the best time is just as the flower has opened. With dried seed pods you can cut when they look brown. Cut the stem as near to the ground as possible. When you have a bundle of stems, tie them together at the bottom and hang them upside down in a dark but airy place. A garden shed is perfect but a cupboard or dark room will do if it is used frequently. True Everlastings, also known as 'immortelles', need no other treatment.

Some other plants are considered valuable in

arrangements and they can be made to be everlasting by the correct use of chemicals. A supplier of the chemicals will also provide instructions on how to do this and advise on which plants to start with. Chemically dried flowers will probably also need new stems as these do not dry well. Replace the stems with pipe-cleaners or florists' wire. For general information including details of local suppliers write to Flora Magazine, Drury House, Russell St, London WC2B 5HD, England, enclosing a stamped addressed envelope or two international reply coupons.

As there are so many Everlastings, I suggest you buy a seed collection and follow the instructions supplied (*Suppliers:* Chiltern Seeds, Thompson and Morgan, Nindethana Seed Service) or you may like to try the following two plants.

The Dwarf Reedmace – Typha minima

A lovely choice, as this has a tall, thin stem with a large head of brown, female flowers. It looks a bit like a fuzzy pipe-cleaner on the end of a stick. Typha (tie-fer) can grow from 40 cm to over 2 m tall. Typha minima is a small species and is therefore easy to grow. It will not flower until there is a lot of it so have a little patience. Flower stalks can be easily cut and dried hanging upside-down.

How to grow

You will need 5–15 cm depth of soil in a pot. Plastic pots designed for use in ponds are best and you should line these with sacking (hessian) before filling them with soil. Plant Typha so that any new shoots are just beneath the soil.

Place the pot in a pond so that it is completely submerged, but not deeper than 24 cm. Any good soil will do. If there are fish in the pond, cover the soil with gravel to prevent it being dug up.

How to get more
Typha will spread quite quickly. All you need to do is pull or cut apart new plants from the others. This is best done in spring.

Suppliers: Stapely Water Gardens or most garden centres selling pond plants. Any other Reedmace or Bullrush may be chosen instead and will look similar

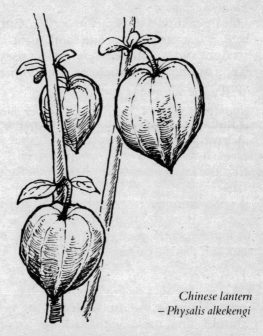

*Chinese lantern
– Physalis alkekengi*

Chinese Lantern – Physalis alkekengi
These are odd plants simply because the flowers are so strange. The fruit or seeds are protected by a

bright orange lantern. They grow 30–100 cm tall but spread very quickly, so watch out.

To dry Physalis (fizz–are–liss), hang them upside down as described above but take off the leaves first. They are ready to be cut for drying when the lantern begins to turn orange.

How to grow
Grow them outdoors in any soil that is reasonably well drained. Add sand to a wet soil. Physalis prefers full sun.

How to get more
Dig up a clump of plants in spring. Cut the clump into pieces using a spade, and plant them again straight away. Alternatively, collect seeds from ripe lanterns and throw these on the soil the following spring.

Suppliers: Beth Chatto. Any good garden centre should have these plants. Seeds from Chiltern Seeds or Thompson and Morgan

13 Plants from the age of the dinosaurs

Plants existed in this world a long time before human beings or any other animals. Many of the plants we see today are descendants of these early plants but most of them have changed during the millions of years their types have existed. However, just as crocodiles are very ancient reptiles that have looked the same for millions of years, there are a few plants that look the same now as they did when dinosaurs walked the earth. They are fascinating and very rare. Most of them are protected in the wild so they can be difficult to get, but they do make beautiful collectors' items.

Cycads – Cycas revoluta and Macrozamia spiralis

Cycads (sigh–cads) have existed for about 150 million years without changing at all. They look quite like ferns except that the leaves are very tough. They all have very large seeds and produce plants that will be anything from 50 cm to several metres wide. They do not usually outgrow a house, though, as they grow incredibly slowly, often producing only one new leaf a year. By growing them in small pots they make excellent Bonsai plants. Cycas revoluta (sigh–cass rev-oh-lute-ah) and Macrozamia spiralis (mac-roe-zame-ee-ah spear-are-liss) are good plants to start with because they are small.

How to grow
Use a pot that is about 3–6 cm wider than the seed. Fill it with any commercial potting compost. To be sure of success you must now sterilize the soil. Buy a

97

fungicide solution from a garden centre and make it up by following the instructions on the packet. Also buy a liquid pesticide and make up some of that. Stand the pot of soil in the liquid fungicide until the top of the soil looks wet. Take the pot out and let it drain for ten minutes. Now soak the pot in the liquid pesticide for five minutes and again drain for ten minutes. Finally, half bury the Cycad seed.

A good supplier should give instructions, but if not, put the pot and seed in a plastic bag, seal and store at 21–23°C (70–75°F) until the seed germinates. Then put the pot in the light and slowly open the bag a little each day. Finally, remove the bag and keep in good light, but never too cold. A greenhouse or windowsill will do. Water the soil whenever it feels dry, but be careful not to over-water in winter. It may take several months for the seed to begin to grow.

How to get more
Buy another seed!

Suppliers: Plants often available at florist shops or good garden centres. Seeds from Chiltern Seeds, Nindethana Seed Service

The Maidenhair Tree – Ginkgo biloba
Ginkgo biloba (gin-coe bi-lobe-ah) is another one of these ancient plants that is reputed to have been a food of the dinosaurs. It certainly is a very ancient plant. Fir trees are older than flowering trees. Ginkgos are related to firs but are even older – in fact they are about 180 million years old.

The trees are hardy but prefer to be warm. They grow quite large so are not often seen in gardens but would make another excellent Bonsai plant. They are more or less like ordinry trees but the leaves are fan-shaped with a frilled edge.

How to grow
Use any soil or commercial potting compost. Keep them protected from frost for the first three years of life and plant outdoors. They like full sun, but should be protected from the summer sun until they are three years old. Water the soil whenever it feels dry. Outdoors, your plant will not need much attention after its first year in the ground.

How to get more
As it is very difficult to produce seed from a Ginkgo, it is best if you get more by buying plants or seed. Seed can be sown on commercial potting compost in spring. Stand the pot of soil in water until the surface is damp. Drain the pot for ten minutes. Sprinkle the seeds on to the soil surface and cover the pot with a plastic bag. Keep the seeds at about 18–23°C (65–75°F) until they germinate. Then gradually remove the bag and keep the seedlings in good but not direct light. Keep the soil moist.

Suppliers: Chiltern Seeds, Hilliers, Plant Shops Botanical

14 Tropical treatment

The first plants to be valued by humans were those which were useful in one or more ways. For instance, the plants producing nuts, berries, or edible roots must have been very familiar to our primitive ancestors. Other plants may have been valued more as material for woven clothes, bags or, perhaps, for building a roof. However, of all the plants of use to a primitive tribe, surely those with a medicinal use must have been most valued. These were the plants that mysteriously enabled a sick person to live and made the medicine man tremendously important, powerful and respected.

These medicine plants were so valuable they could not be left behind when a tribe moved. While food plants were quite easy to discover in a new place, it is not easy to look at a plant and know if it will heal or not. So very early on in history people began to carry medicine plants with them on long journeys. Wherever they have lived there are usually medicine plants nearby and the Aloe is just one of them that has taken up residence on a small but popular island.

The Medicinal Aloe – Aloe barbadensis (now usually called Aloe vera)

Aloe barbadensis (al-oh bar-bah-den-sis) is so named because it is now found in Barbados, an island so far to the west of the Atlantic Ocean that most people think it is in the Caribbean. In fact it doesn't matter because, although it is not a true Caribbean island, it does have a typically tropical climate and the beautiful beaches you expect in the tropics.

The tourists go there to enjoy the weather and usually go home feeling healthier as a result of having a good time. One or two go home with varying degrees of sunburn. Various creams are sold that purport to relieve the pain, but little do the tourists know they have left the best remedy behind them.

The juice of the Medicinal Aloe, obtained by breaking a leaf in half and squeezing it, is well known to doctors as a very good treatment for burns. Although cold water is the best thing to put on a burn, the water will only take the heat out of it and prevent scarring if done quickly. What the water cannot do, but the aloe can is to speed up the healing process. So, if you have been burnt and you want it to heal quickly, you can put a little Aloe barbadensis juice on the burn and it should take less time to heal. But DO SEE A DOCTOR.

The Medicinal Aloe is so good at healing burns that the American army have got thousands of them. In the event of a war there would be many people suffering from burns and they hope to be able to heal most of them with Aloe juice.

Whether or not that will be necessary, Barbados is still the home of this interesting plant and therefore must be quite a healthy place to visit.

How to grow

Aloes are usually very large but, as they are slow growers, the seedlings are excellent house plants. They will not survive a frost, so in temperate climates they must be grown indoors or in a green-house. You will need a pot that is just wider than your plant, about 7–30 cm wide. Fill it with John Innis No. 2 or any commercial potting compost with some added sand and grit. In summer, plant outdoors in full sun and give plenty of water as often as possible. In winter, keep at about 5°C (41°F) and give very little water, no more than once a month unless the weather turns warm.

How to get more

Mature plants will produce new, young plants (off-sets) on their side. These can be pulled off, the broken end painted with a little nail varnish and then planted in another pot. Seeds can be grown quite easily if you begin in spring. Get a plastic container with drainage holes in the bottom and fill it with the soil. Stand the container in water until the soil looks wet and then let it drain for ten minutes. Sprinkle seeds on the soil surface and cover them with a thin layer of fine gravel. (Do not worry if you have no gravel. It is helpful but not essential.) Finally, cover the container in a plastic bag to keep in the moisture. Now keep this at 21°C (70°F) until the seeds have germinated.

Repot the seedlings only when they have grown sufficiently that they are about to touch the plastic bag. If the bag is used properly you will not need to water the soil at all until you repot. If it does look dry, carefully stand the container in a little water for five minutes without the plastic film, drain for ten minutes and then recover. Seedling will appreciate good light but not direct sunlight.

Suppliers: Abbeybrook, Plant Shops Botanical

All the suppliers listed below are well known and highly recommended. They all have a reputation for supplying excellent plants or seeds and should all replace any goods that are unsatisfactory. They should also be happy to answer enquiries as long as you send them a stamped and addressed envelope (or two international reply coupons if you are overseas). Unless stated otherwise, you should send 50p (British Nurseries) or four international reply coupons if you want to have a plant or seed catalogue sent to you. If you live outside Britain and want to obtain a catalogue from a local nursery send them the equivalent of $1.

All suppliers are in England unless stated otherwise.

Abbeybrook Cactus Nursery, Old Hackney Lane, Matlock, Derbyshire

If you cannot find an interesting plant in this list then you probably have not read it properly. An enormous choice of cacti and other succulents available both as plants or seed.

Avon Bulbs, Bathford, Bath BA1 8ED

Very large selection of beautiful and interesting bulbs. Order quickly or well in advance as this nursery is very popular and the really interesting plants can sell out very quickly.

Barleyfield Nursery, Southburgh (Nr Hingham), Thetford, Norfolk

Specialist supplier of succulents including cacti. An amazing assortment, including several you might like that are not listed in this book.

Beckwood Geraniums, Beckwood Nurseries Ltd, New Inn Road, Beckley, Nr Oxford

A specialist supplier of Geraniums and Pelargoniums with something to please everyone.

**Beth Chatto, White Barn House, Elmstead
Market, Colchester, Essex**

The catalogue of plants includes other useful
information on which plants will grow under special
conditions.

**Carnivorous Gardens, PO Box 224, Stones
Corner 4120, Brisbane, Queensland, Australia**

Seeds of Australian carnivorous plants.

**Chiltern Seeds, Bortree Stile,
Cumbria LA12 7PB**

The best seed catalogue in the world. The list of
seeds is enormous but the descriptions are pure
entertainment, well worth reading. Well over 1,000
different species supplied.

**P. J. Christian, Pentre Cottages, Minera,
Clwyd, N. Wales**

A specialist nursery that has a smaller list of plants
than most of those listed but many will not be available anywhere else. Definitely a nursery that all keen
collectors should know about.

**Hillier's Nursery, Ampfield House, Ampfield,
Romsey, Hants**

One of the largest nurseries in the world. An enormous selection of trees, shrubs and other plants.
Catalogue is 30p or four international reply
coupons.

**Hinode-Kadan Nursery, 2735 Nakanogo,
Hacijyot, Hachijyo-Island, Tokyo 100–16,
Japan**

Large list of carnivorous plants, many available
nowhere else.

Holly Gate Cactus Nursery, Billinghurst Lane, Ashington, West Sussex RH20 3BA

An excellent selection of plants and seed, including both cacti and other succulents.

P. Kohli, Park Road, Near Neelam Theatre, Srinagar, Kashmir, India

Supplier of native Indian plants as seeds or bulbs. Particularly useful for aroids and some dwarf bulbs.

Marston Exotics, Spring Gardens, Frome, Somerset

All types of carnivorous plants to choose from a large list. They also provide a very useful beginner's guide or catalogue.

Milingimbi Nursery, PO Box 5, Seaforth, NSW, Australia 2092

Australian carnivorous plant nursery offering plants from around the world but specializing in plants and advice for the beginner.

New Dawn Nurseries, 50 Knightsbridge Avenue, Valley View, SA 5093, Australia

Various carnivorous plants available grown in test tubes. Good Australian supplier as people resident in South Australia will find it difficult to import plants from out-of-state or overseas.

Nindethana Seed Service, Narrikup 6326, Western Australia, Australia

Plenty of 'Everlasting' Australian plants available as seed with many other Australian species of interest. Unfortunately, the plants are not described so you will need a book describing Australian plants.

Oak Garden, Kuguno-Cho, Gifu-Ken 509-32, Japan

A smaller list than many but every plant is a gem.

The aroids are difficult to obtain elsewhere so for these alone the list is useful. Many other plants will be unusual outside Japan.

Renate Parsley, 8 Langton Road, Mowbray 7700, South Africa

Seeds of South African carnivorous plants.

Peter Paul's Nurseries, Canandaigua, NY 14424, USA

Plants and seeds of carnivorous plants. Catalogue $0.50.

Plant Shop's Botanical Garden, 18007 Topham Street, Reseda, CA 91335, USA

A massive list of various types of plant including aroids, succulents and carnivorous plants. Excellent if you live in the USA but there is a minimum export order of $100. The catalogue is $2 but is refunded if you order any plants.

Sandwich Nurseries, Dover Road, Sandwich, Kent CT13 0DG

A delightful catalogue full of useful plants, many of which have unusual smells.

Sarracenia Nurseries, Links Side, Courtland Avenue, Mill Hill, London NW7

Good list of carnivorous plants from around the world. Several may be available as seed as well. A discount is given to members of the Carnivorous Plant Society. Suppliers are: Thompson and Morgan, London Road, Ipswich, Suffolk IP2 0BA.

Stapely Water Gardens Ltd, London Road, Stapely, Nantwich, Cheshire

The largest supplier of water plants (and also fish pond liners etc.) in Britain.

Thysanotus-Seed-Mailorder, Postfach 44-8109, 2800 Bremen 44, West Germany

German supplier of carnivorous plant seeds.

Valhalla Research, Lane, Kommetjie 7976, South Africa

A massive list of plants including carnivores, Aroids Osbourne (Araceae), Air Plants, Prayer Plants and one or two other oddities. Outside of South Africa the minimum order is, unfortunately, $100.

Vesutor Ltd, The Bromeliad Nursery, Billinghurst Lane, Ashington, West Sussex RH20 3BA

The specialist nursery for Bromeliads in Britain. A very large and ever-increasing selection of plants of the pineapple family including the amazing Air Plants. Very helpful to beginners and a very readable catalogue.

Harald Weiner Dipl. Ing., Kaiserstrasse 74, 3250 Hameln 1, West Germany

The largest European supplier of carnivorous plants with very competitive prices and a choice of all the easier plants to grow and many rarer types. No collector of carnivorous plants can afford not to see this list from time to time.

16   Useful societies

These are just a few of the societies that you can join or write to. Please remember that they receive hundreds of enquiries and that can be expensive. It helps them if you always enclose a stamped and addressed envelope (or two international reply coupons) whenever you write to them.

The Carnivorous Plant Society, The Secretary, 174 Baldwins Lane, Croxley Green, Herts WD3 3LQ

The British society with members from all over the world. Members can get free advice on anything to do with carnivorous plants, including addresses of other societies. A journal is produced twice a year and a newsletter quarterly. Seeds of many species are available free of charge and plants can often be obtained from other members for a very small charge. Meetings are held once a month in London.

The Australian Carnivorous Plant Society, PO Box 256, Goodwood, S. Australia, Australia

Another society for carnivorous plant enthusiasts. Very similar to the others, but it is in Australia. Useful to belong to even if you do not live there.

Brisbane Carnivorous Plant Society PO Box 320, Archerfield, Q 4108, Queensland, Australia.

Australia is a big place. It is best to belong to a local society, so this is one for people living in Queensland. Newsletters, seeds and a plant exchange for collectors of carnivorous plants. Also meetings, advice and competitions.

International Carnivorous Plant Society, The Fullerton Arboretum, California State University, Fullerton, CA 92634, USA

Another carnivorous plant society but this time in America. No meetings but they can give addresses of local societies in America where meetings are held. A quarterly colour journal and seeds are available to members.

New Zealand Carnivorous Plant Society, 561 Harewood Street, Christchurch 5, Christchurch, New Zealand

Another society for readers in New Zealand – again offering newsletters, seeds and plant exchanges.

The Royal Horticultural Society, Vincent Square, London SW1P 2PE

A society for all people interested in plants. They will supply information to non-members but members will receive a monthly journal and a chance to obtain some of the seeds offered from the winter list. Certainly worth writing to if you do not know a society near you, as they will probably know if there is one.

The Cactus and Succulent Society of Great Britain, The Honourable Secretary, Miss W. E. Dunn, 43 Dewar Drive, Sheffield

For all those interested in these very collectable plants. There are meetings, journals, free seeds and plenty of advice. Their information booklet costs 65p (four international reply coupons or $1 if you are overseas).

The British Pelargonium and Geranium Society, 2/108 Rosendale Road, London SE21

They provide members with a yearbook, three journals, seeds and advice, as well as holding meetings all over the country.

Index